THE BOOK OF

TEA

AND

HERBS

The REPUBLIC of TEA

THE BOOK OF

T E A

AND

H E R B S

**APPRECIATING THE VARIETALS
AND VIRTUES OF
FINE TEA AND HERBS**

A PRACTICAL GUIDE FROM THE
MINISTRY OF INFORMATION

Published by

THE COLE GROUP

4415 SONOMA HIGHWAY, SANTA ROSA, CA 95409

800-959-2717 VOICE 707-538-0492 FAX 707-538-0497

Book design by

GINA AMADOR

The information and suggestions in this book are presented as topics of general interest and are not intended to replace the recommendations of a qualified health professional. Any application of information, suggestions, preparations, or procedures in this book is at the reader's risk and any adverse effects or consequences are the reader's sole responsibility.

Library of Congress Catalog Card Number 93-31073

ISBN 1-56426-570-6

Printed and Bound in Canada

A B C D E F G
3 4 5 6 7 8 9 0

Distributed to the book trade by Publisher's Group West

DEDICATED TO THE MEMORY OF
WILLIAM H. UKERS (1873-1954),
HONORARY MINISTER OF PROPAGANDA,
WHO PAVED THE PATH OF TEA
FROM PAST TO PRESENT,
AND WHOSE SPIRIT INFUSES
EVERY PAGE OF THIS BOOK.

CONTENTS

SECTION II: HERBS

**REFLECTIONS ON MY REFLECTION
IN A CUP OF TEA**

WITH EACH SIP I TASTE
THE FIRE THAT GIVES ITS HEAT,
THE WATER THAT GIVES ITS WETNESS,
THE LEAF THAT GIVES ITS SPELL,
THE POT THAT GIVES ITS EMPTINESS.

WITH EACH LINGERING SIP
I CANNOT HELP BUT SEE
ALL THAT MAKES TEA
AS WELL MAKES ME.

– The Minister of Leaves

Dear Fellow People of Tea,

What is tea?

Where does tea come from?

How is tea good for health?

What are the best ways to brew and appreciate tea?

How is "herb tea" different from black or green tea?

Which herbs make the most delicious "herb teas"?

In our travels outside the Republic of Tea, we have heard these questions many times. In the spirit of public service, we decided it was time to share the answers.

This book, originally intended for our Republic's ambassadors, is a guide to the beguiling mysteries of the brewable leaves – tea from the *Camellia sinensis* bush, and herbs from a host of other useful and flavorful plants.

Every book, like every cup of tea, is a journey of discovery. On behalf of the Republic of Tea, I invite you to discover yourself among the leaves of this one.

Progress

The Minister of Progress

T E A

TEA IS THE TEACHER.
BEING IS THE TEACHING.

– *The Minister of Leaves*

CHAPTER 1

An Introduction to the Plant, the Leaf, and the Manufacture of Tea

*A Definition - The Tea Belt - How Climate and
Elevation Affect Tea - The Flush - Tea Varietals
Two Leaves and a Bud - Does Leaf Size Matter?
Black, Green, and Oolong - Grading Tea
Blended and Scented Teas - Tea Bags
How Tea Is Sold - The Price of Tea
Two Methods of Making Tea - Tasting Tea
Storing Tea - Fresh Tea Is Hard To Find*

Camellia sinensis

Tea: A Definition

There are many teas, but only one plant.

That plant is **Camellia sinensis,** a relative of the flowering camellia well known to gardeners. Incredible as it seems, the few leaves that sprout at the very top of this plant, and this plant only, are what is transformed into *all* types of tea – black, green, and Oolong. (*Camellia sinensis* leaves are not the source of "herb teas," properly known as infusions, which are discussed in Section Two.) The leaves contain caffeine, and so do all the teas made from them, in varying amounts.

One plant...many teas. How can it be? This is the fascinating mystery of tea. To understand it, consider a comparison to wine. One species, *Vitis vinifera,* is responsible for nearly all the wine drunk in the world. Yet no conscientious student would mistake a delicate white Chardonnay for a robust Pinot Noir or an effervescent Champagne. So it is with tea.

As with wine grapes, subtle differences of soil, elevation, and climate all affect the character of tea leaves. The whims of weather cycles – early monsoon, late monsoon, drought – are also crucial. And a great deal of tea's character comes from the choice of leaves picked and how they are treated, or "**manufactured**," after they are plucked from the branches.

Tea is an evergreen shrub. In the wild, it may grow as tall as 60 feet or taller.

When cultivated for harvest, the tea bush is continually pruned to about three feet (five feet if it is to be subjected to the lamentable practice of mechanical harvesting). From the air, the plantings resemble a dense green mat, faintly furrowed by the narrow, serpentine paths between the bushes. Even if it spans hundreds of acres, a tea plantation is called a **garden**.

ancient wild tea tree

The Tea Belt: Where Tea Grows

Tea is indigenous to that part of the world we now call China, Tibet, and northern India. Over the centuries, it has been transplanted far and wide, and today is successfully cultivated within a geographic belt that runs from the equator to 42° north.

Tea is commercially cultivated in places as diverse as Russia, Kenya, and Argentina. It thrived experimentally in South Carolina for 25 years around the turn of the nineteenth century (but proved too expensive to produce commercially). The great teas of the world, however, come from a handful of countries – most prominently CHINA, FORMOSA (TAIWAN), CEYLON (SRI LANKA), JAPAN, and INDIA.

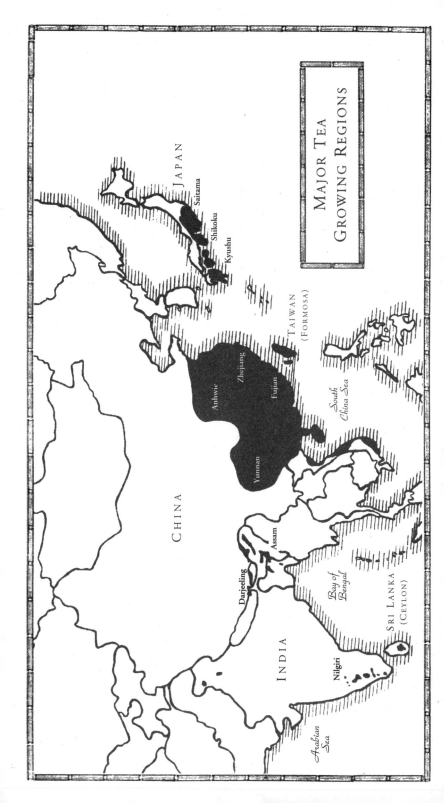

MAJOR TEA
GROWING REGIONS

JAPAN
Saitama
Shikoku
Kyushu

TAIWAN
(FORMOSA)

CHINA

Anhwie
Zhejiang
Fujian
Yunnan

South
China Sea

Darjeeling
Assam

Bay of
Bengal

INDIA

Nilgiri

SRI LANKA
(CEYLON)

Arabian
Sea

How Climate and Elevation Affect Tea

A hardy bush, the tea plant thrives in tropical and subtropical climates with warm temperatures, plenty of shade (usually supplied by carefully selected shade trees), and abundant rainfall of 80 to 100 inches a year. Seasonal monsoon rains, which bring torrential rains and temperatures of up to 95°F, inspire the leaves' growth spurts.

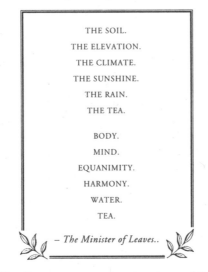

THE SOIL.

THE ELEVATION.

THE CLIMATE.

THE SUNSHINE.

THE RAIN.

THE TEA.

BODY.

MIND.

EQUANIMITY.

HARMONY.

WATER.

TEA.

– The Minister of Leaves..

The finest teas grow at elevations of 3,000 to 6,000 feet, in a relatively cooler climate that slows the growth of the leaves. Slight differences in elevation can produce remarkable differences in the size and quality of the leaf. The mountainous terrain in DARJEELING, in northern India, and the hilly gardens of CEYLON require intricate patchworks of plantings that curve along mountain slopes.

The Flush

The sprouting of new leaves and buds on the tea bush is called a *flush*. Tea plants may flush two, three, or more times within the growing season. In JAVA and SUMATRA, where there is no cold season, tea flushes all year round and may be plucked every seven to ten days. In drier, mountainous areas tea gardens may produce only a single flush each season.

The most famous "flushes" come from Darjeeling, where each flush has its own distinct character and the first flush in the early spring is celebrated like the release of nouveau Beaujolais wine in France. (For more about Darjeeling flushes, please see Chapter Four in this Section.)

Tea Varietals

Camellia sinensis reproduces by *cross-pollination* – pollen is transferred from the flowers of one plant to those of another. Because in nature this process yields random results, commercial growers produce tea plants either from seedlings – the cheap and efficient method – or through cuttings from a desirable parent plant – the superior but more laborious method.

Some 2,000 varietals of tea – distinct sub-species with their own appearance and characters – have been identified and cultivated.

Different growing areas are known for specific tea varietals, rather as different grape-growing areas are known for their varietal wines such as Pinot Noir or Chardonnay. (There are more teas in China than there are wines in France!) A tea connoisseur can identify a tea varietal by its leaf size, shape, color, and fragrance. Some varietals produce outstanding beverages on their own; others are best in blends.

Two Leaves and a Bud

fine

medium

coarse

plucking diagram

Although a tea bush needs to be at least three years old and three feet tall before it's harvested, tea pluckers look only at the uppermost inch or two, where the youngest, most tender leaves are found. Fine, full-leaf teas are made only from these young shoots, at most a single bud and two leaves.

For centuries, perhaps millennia, tea was harvested and processed only by hand in what is called the "**orthodox**" method. Where quality is paramount, and the full-leaf is respected, it still is. The process is beautiful to watch: The harvesters, usually women in colorful saris and straw hats or white headcloths, wind gracefully through the bushes, nipping off the topmost inch with their fingernails and dropping the leaves into baskets on their backs. They are paid according to the weight and the quality of the leaves they pick.

Twentieth-century haste, under the twin banners of Efficiency and Convenience, has increasingly brought harvesting machines into the garden. These machines are indiscriminate, snatching not only the traditional two leaves and a bud but often the entire branch, twigs and all.

tea harvester

Thus rudely ripped from its place of repose, the tea is subjected to further mechanical insults in the form of tearing and crushing. The result is stuffed into tea bags. Quite understandably, the initials **CTC**, industry jargon for this "**Cut-Torn-Crushed**" process, evoke a shudder from lovers of the leaf.

Does Leaf Size Matter?

Before they are processed, tea leaves vary dramatically in size. The fanciest **Formosan** and **Chinese Oolongs** are made from very large leaves that curl during processing but open intact when infused with boiling water. At the other extreme, **Keemun**, the celebrated black tea of ANHWEI, China, is made from camellia plants having a natu-

rally small, compact leaf. Within each varietal's natural range, teas are graded according to the size of their leaf, and the general rule of thumb is: THE LARGER THE LEAF, THE MORE DISTINCT THE FLAVOR.

Black, Green, and Oolong

Darjeeling (black)

Gu Zhang Mao Jian
(green)

Formosa Oolong

Whether a tea leaf ends up being called black (fermented), green (unfermented), or Oolong (semi-fermented) is determined during the process of manufacture. Tea manufacture is by and large a matter of skilled manual labor.

BLACK TEA. To create black tea (or red tea, as it is known in China for the beautiful liquor color it produces), the leaves are plucked and then treated in a four-step process:

• *Withering* removes moisture from the freshly plucked leaf so that it can be rolled. Leaves are spread uniformly on trays or racks in a cool room for 18 to 24 hours. By the end of this stage, the leaves have lost one-third to one-half of their weight through evaporation and are soft and pliable.

• *Rolling* the leaf, the second step, readies it for transformation. Fine, first-grade teas are rolled by hand, painstakingly curling each leaf longitudinally, twisting it slightly in the process. This breaks apart the cells in the leaf, releasing enzymes that will interact with air and cause oxidation, also known as fermentation. Also, twisted leaves release their flavor more slowly when they are infused. Many teas are now machine-rolled – it is 70 times faster than the hand method. But hand-rolling preserves the "**tip**," which is regarded as a sign of quality .

hand-rolling tea

•*Fermentation* changes the chemical structure of the tea leaf, allowing key flavor characteristics to emerge. (It does not, however, make tea an alcoholic beverage.) The rolled leaves are spread on cement or tile floors and tables in a cool, humid room. They are carefully monitored for the next one to five hours for proper color and pungency. Generally, the longer the leaf ferments, the softer its taste and deeper its color.

•*Firing* is the step that stops fermentation. The leaves are placed in hot pans similar to woks, or in large modern dryers where a constant temperature of 120°F can be maintained. The leaves turn black and lose all but three percent of their original moisture. Improper firing can cause off-color, a loss of flavor and aroma, blistering, mold, and spoilage.

Finally, the tea is sorted, graded, and packed in wooden chests that have been lined with foil to prevent the intrusion of unwelcome flavors and aromas.

GREEN TEA. Leaves intended for green tea are plucked in the same manner as black tea. They are then manufactured in three stages completed within a single day:

•*Panfiring* (or steaming) occurs immediately after the leaves are plucked. The leaves are placed in a metal pan over a hot flame to render them soft and pliable. The sudden exposure to heat destroys the enzymes that would otherwise lead to fermentation.

Chinese firing pan

•*Rolling* the leaves on heated trays to reduce their moisture content is the next step. The process is done with the fingers and palms, and sometimes with the entire forearm up to the elbow.

•*Firing* in large mechanical dryers is the final stage of drying. Fired green tea retains only two percent of its moisture. Some green teas produced for export are rolled and fired several times; although this increases their shelf life, it may also impair their taste and character.

Green tea is then sorted by leaf size and packed. The finest and most delicate grades are often put into metal tins or vacuum-packed to preserve their freshness.

OOLONG. This process, whose name in Chinese means "black dragon," is a relative newcomer in tea manufacture, developed in Formosa only in the mid-nineteenth century. It combines elements of both fermented and unfermented processes. The leaves are picked just as they reach their peak and processed immediately.

• *Withering* and a brief fermentation are combined, for a total of four to five hours in direct sunlight. The leaves are spread three or four inches deep in large bamboo baskets and shaken frequently to bruise the leaf edges, making them oxidize faster than the centers. This stage is halted when the leaves give off a characteristic fragrance, often compared to apples, orchids, or peaches.

• *Firing* halts fermentation when it is about half complete. Baskets full of leaves are moved in and out of the flames of a charcoal fire.

Finally, the tea is sorted for size and color and packed into foil-lined wooden chests for transport.

traditional method of transportation

How Tea Is Graded

Black, green, or Oolong, the tea is now almost ready to be packed away in chests and shipped for sale. First, though, it is *sorted* – sifted by machine or by hand to determine its size: whole leaf, broken/small leaf, fannings, or dust. **Whole leaf** is large and intact; **broken** or **small leaf tea** may be either a smaller grade or slightly torn; **fannings** are even smaller fragments of leaf; and **dust** is whatever is left over from processing.

whole leaves   fannings   dust

Tea is also *graded* according to its quality. Fine-quality black tea is characterized by its "tip." The tips of the leaves do not add to the flavor of tea, but their presence indicates that the leaves were plucked in the orthodox method when very young, then withered and rolled carefully. Some finished tea leaves have a golden or silvery color on one tip. They generally have a very special, complex taste.

There is no universal system of grading tea, so a leaf may well receive one grade in China, another in Ceylon, and a third in India.

Pekoe. One result of this crazy-quilt of standards is a puzzling grading expression, *"pekoe."* The term, which rhymes with "gecko" (not "Rico"), comes from the Chinese word for "white hair," describing the downy tips of young leaf buds. Yet it is used to describe only Indian and Ceylon teas, never Chinese. And it refers not to down or tips but rather to the presence of whole leaves. *"Orange pekoe,"* another frequently used (and misleading) term, has nothing to do with color or flavor. Early Dutch traders used it to imply nobility – it refers to the Dutch House of Orange. Both "pekoe" and "Orange pekoe" are often misused on tea labels to imply flavor rather than as an indication of actual quality.

TEA GRADING AND TERMINOLOGY:
An Abbreviated Glossary

Orange Pekoe (OP) A fancy grade of full-leaf tea showing no tip, but nice thin leaves rolled lengthwise.

Tippy Golden Flowery Orange Pekoe (TGFOP) The absolute top grade, usually assigned only to full-leaf Indian teas from Darjeeling and Assam. Slightly lesser leaves receive fewer letters (**GFOP, FOP**). Occasionally the numeral "1" or "2" will follow the letters, signifying an even finer grading among similar leaves.

Broken Orange Pekoe (BOP) A broken or smaller leaf; a step below the full leaf. Can also be characterized as "tippy," "golden," "flowery" or any combination of those terms.

Fannings (F) Very small broken leaves about the size of a pinhead. Fannings may be produced by either orthodox or CTC methods. CTC fannings are chunkier in shape.

Dust (D) Literally the bottom of the chest or barrel. The smallest broken leaf left over in the manufacturing and sifting process. Also known as **"sweepings"** (although, contrary to rumor, not swept off the floor).

Pekoe Fannings (PF) and Pekoe Dust (PD) Both terms describe teas produced using the CTC method specifically for better-quality tea bags. They are grainy or even chunky, infuse and color quickly, and tend to be quite aromatic.

Green teas are graded in a different manner. The highest-quality green teas consist of a bud and one leaf, followed in descending order by a bud and two leaves, a bud and three leaves, and so on.

Blended Teas

Most packaged tea sold in stores outside our Republic, whether loose or in tea bags, is a blend of many different teas harvested from different flushes in different estates – even different countries. The concept is not new. In the 1700s and 1800s, it was fashionable to store different varietals of fine unblended tea leaves in separate tea caddies and blend them in the pot – for instance, Assam from India and Keemun from China for a brisk breakfast blend.

Partly to suit this acquired taste, and partly because the quality and taste of leaves from a single tea garden vary from crop to crop and season to season, tea merchants began blending their products to "smooth out" their inherent variations and to overcome shortages created by seasonal production and poor harvests. This practice is directly comparable to the practice of vintners who blend grapes from several vineyards to produce an acceptable, but undistinguished, "generic" wine.

In the seventeenth through nineteenth centuries, unscrupulous tea blenders sometimes mixed their product with dried, used tea leaves, leaves from other plants, or even sawdust. This practice eventually led to laws that protect citizens from adulterated teas.

THE UNITED STATES TEA ACT OF 1897 was passed to ensure quality and purity standards and fitness for consumption of all teas imported into the United States. Originally intended to protect consumers from inferior-quality dust teas that had been "masked" or cut with non-tea ingredients, the act has been amended several times but remains in force today. The U.S. Government still maintains a small **Board of Tea Experts and Tea Examiners**, responsible for inspecting every shipment of tea that enters the United States.

The Invention of Tea Bags

The tea bag was invented in America as a marketing gambit in 1908, when tea merchant JOHN SULLIVAN decided to distribute his samples in hand-sewn cloth sacks. Those bags contained fine-quality full-leaf teas and customers discovered they could put the samples, bags and all, directly into tea pots. The bags were just large enough to let the leaves fully expand and infuse properly.

tea sack

Customers enjoyed the pre-measured bags, which were convenient and simplified removal of leaves from the tea pot.

Sullivan's unwitting innovation led to the most damaging development in modern tea history: the single-serve tea bag.

To brew a single cup of tea, as opposed to a pot, requires a smaller tea bag, which in turn requires smaller leaves to facilitate proper brewing. This was a boon to restaurants, which generally serve hot water at 190°F – significantly lower than the boiling point of 212°F needed to properly infuse full-leaf tea. Only a tea bag filled with tea dust will produce a dark, strong-tasting cup in water below the boiling point.

However, using smaller leaves or leaf fragments (fannings or dust) means compromising the taste of the full leaf.

As demand for tea bags increased, tea growers produced greater yields of lesser-quality tea that could be cut, torn, crushed, and stuffed into packets.

THERE IS THE SIZE OF THE LEAF,
ITS UNIQUE SHAPE,
ITS UNIQUE COLOR,
ITS UNIQUE FRAGRANCE,
A TASTE ALL ITS OWN,
AND IT CHANGES... SIP BY SIP.

– *The Minister of Leaves*

How Tea Is Sold

After tea has been graded, it is packed into chests that weigh between 40 and 75 pounds each. The chests are assigned to lots (or *chops*); although the chests aren't standard in weight, the chops are.

A chop, or seal, identifies an individual, a family, or a trademark. By extension, it also refers to an entire batch, or lot, of tea.

Envelopes of leaf samples are distributed throughout the world to buyers and brokers who *cup* the teas – taste them and compare their smell, taste, and appearance to those of other teas and to general standards.

The tea is then "**offered**" directly to the buyer or contributed to an auction list where it will be sold with other chops of teas. Auctions are held weekly in LONDON and CALCUTTA.

The finest teas are produced in very limited quantities of as little as 200 kilograms (three to five chests), which translates to about 2,000 individual tins of tea. They are often purchased immediately – or even by advance bid, as with wine futures.

The Price of Tea

Fine, full-leaf teas are priced by their growers and are not subject to negotiation. They may fetch between $8 and $60 a kilogram, or even more. Once in a while, as with fine wine, an extraordinary tea comes along and commands a price some would call outrageous...but which seems entirely logical to the overjoyed buyer.

Average-quality teas, considered more of a commodity like soybeans or coffee, are sold at auction. They may cost as little as $1 a kilogram.

Chinese tea caddy

Today, fine tea is a very affordable luxury, especially when calculated by the cost per cup. A pound of leaf tea will produce about 200 cups, so even a very rare tea priced at $100 a pound costs a mere 50 cents per cup.

Brewing Tea

Preparing tea for drinking is one of life's simplest and most satisfying pleasures. Yet making a pot of full-leaf tea (without the aid of tea bags) remains a challenge to many new arrivals to the Republic, not to mention the millions still stranded outside our borders.

In fact, making tea is as simple as you want it to be. Here are two approaches, one explicit, one intuitive. Choose one or discover a path of your own.

THE MINISTER OF PROGRESS'S METHOD

Some tea lovers say one should keep a minimum of three tea pots – one for black tea, one for green tea, and one for scented blends – but others make fine tea with a single humble pot. In any case, take care not to clean the tea pot with scouring powders, or even soap or detergent; a good rinse with clean water will suffice.

WATER QUALITY IS IMPORTANT. The subtler the flavor of the tea, the more influence the taste of the water will have. If you're dissatisfied with the tea you've brewed, the fault may lie not in the leaves but in the water's impurities. Try a good-quality bottled water, or filter your tap water, to experience an improvement.

WATER TEMPERATURE IS IMPORTANT. Black tea should be made with water that has been brought to a full rolling boil and then immediately poured into the pot or cup. Green tea, which is more delicate and subtle, responds best to water that has been brought just up to the boiling point, no further.

UTENSILS CAN MAKE A DIFFERENCE. The pot, infuser, and cup contribute to the overall experience of your brew.

Before adding leaves or boiling water, warm the pot by swishing around a little hot water inside it.

HOW MUCH TEA? Use about one level teaspoon of full-leaf tea per cup (1.5 to 2 grams). British tea

continued on p. 36

THE MINISTER OF LEAVES' METHOD

BOIL WATER.

INFUSE LEAVES.

DRINK TEA.

merchants invented the notion of adding "a tea-spoon for the pot" to create a stronger tea that would be diluted with milk (and perhaps to sell more tea as well).

HOW LONG TO INFUSE? The typical infusion for full-leaf black tea should last four to five minutes. Green teas, and smaller-leaf black teas, require less time – about three minutes. Fine Oolong teas, with their very large leaves, can brew for seven to ten minutes without becoming bitter. On the other hand, tea bags, filled with fannings or dust, infuse very quickly – sometimes in as little as 30 seconds. A rule of thumb: the smaller the leaf, the faster the infusion.

REMOVING THE LEAVES FROM THE LIQUID at the proper time is important to avoid overbrewing or "stewing" the leaves. This is easily accomplished by pouring the tea through a mesh or bamboo strainer, or by using a teapot with a removable infusing basket that fits inside the neck of the pot. The latter makes it particularly easy to remove the used leaves from the pot, allowing for the enjoyment of a second cup. Infusers also simplify clean-up and disposal of the leaves. If you use a wire-mesh tea ball, take care to fill it only halfway, as the leaves will double in size as they steep. (Avoid perforated metal "eggs" – not enough water can circulate around the leaves.)

HOW MANY INFUSIONS? Black teas lend themselves to a single infusion, and are discarded after an individual cup or pot is made. Most green teas are also used just once, although some are suited to several consecutive swift (one-minute) infusions. Finer Oolong teas are generally infused a couple of times, and may even be infused as many as seven times using the same leaves. The Chinese say you derive different pleasures from each successive infusion.

❧❧

The first bowl sleekly moistened throat and lips,
The second banished all my loneliness
The third expelled the dullness from my mind,
Sharpening inspiration gained
from all the books I've read.
The fourth brought forth light perspiration,
Dispersing a lifetime's troubles through my pores.
The fifth bowl cleansed ev'ry atom of my being.
The sixth has made me kin to the Immortals.
This seventh is the utmost I can drink –
A light breeze issues from my armpits.

– FROM "THE SONG OF TEA," LU T'UNG, CHINESE POET,
EIGHTH CENTURY A.D.

TWO METHODS FOR MAKING ICED TEA

A. Prepare a double-strength infusion of hot tea. Strain and let cool to room temperature. Pour into glasses filled with ice cubes.

B. This method requires a bit more of a wait but produces a clearer liquid. Prepare a regular-strength infusion using cold water instead of boiling water. Stir well and refrigerate overnight. Stir again. Serve without ice.

Tasting Tea

Only the tea-drinker can say whether the tea is well made. Nevertheless, a few general guidelines apply.

Leaf. To repeat, the larger the leaf, the better...in general. Tea buyers look for the presence of tip (golden or silver, suggesting that very young leaves were used), consistency, and evenness. They also evaluate the twist of the rolled leaf; "wiry" and "well-twisted" are favorable terms.

Liquor. This has to do not with alcoholic spirits but rather with the color of the infusion. Tea tasters assess clarity, brightness of color, and general aesthetic appearance. Fine black teas are sometimes classified as "coppery" or "bright" in appearance.

Aroma. The "nose" of a tea says a lot about its age. Older teas lose their lively natural fragrance over time. With a little experience, one can learn to detect subtle variations of fragrance. A smoky aroma is called "tarry"; a well-fired Assam tea may be said to smell "biscuity." Ordinary green tea has comparatively little aroma to black tea.

professional tasting cup (tea infuses for 4-5 minutes)

tasting cup is then tipped into bowl

Taste. "Clean" and "brisk" are desirable; "flat," "dull," and "sweaty" are objectionable. Tasters seek complex flavor characteristics – flowery, woody, malty, pungent – and evaluate the tea's body or strength. A critical factor is the leaf's lack of harshness: the finer (and, usually, the younger) the leaf, the mellower the infusion.

quality of leaves and liquor is noted before tasting

Milk and Sugar

Milk in tea is a western European invention, introduced by the Dutch in the early 1600s and popularized in France a century later. The custom took hold in Great Britain in the 1800s, where milk was used to soften the "edge," or astringency, of robust black teas from China and India. (Neither milk nor sugar is used in China, or with green teas anywhere.)

The preferred British fashion is "**MIF**," or "**Milk In First.**" A few drops of warm milk are poured into the cup, followed by the tea. (There is a practical historical reason for this practice: It kept the scalding tea from cracking fragile porcelain cups.) The British also adopted the custom of sweetening their tea with a generous amount of sugar. After QUEEN VICTORIA visited Russia (her daughter's adopted country), Britons began offering an alternative to milk: slices of lemon, in the Russian manner.

In Tibet, tea is customarily churned with yak butter and other ingredients (sometimes crushed walnut meat, peanuts, egg, salt, or sugar) to yield a thick beverage called **tsampa**.

tsampa churner

Storing Tea

The taste of tea deteriorates over time as the essential oils – the volatile compounds that give tea its fragrance – evaporate from the leaves. Most well-manufactured black teas will remain flavorful for 18 to 24 months from the time they were harvested. Delicate, first-flush teas, like those from Darjeeling, lose their best notes only a few months after picking. Cut fannings and tea dust used in tea bags tend to go stale even faster. (**Keemun**, an exception here as elsewhere, seems to develop new flavor characteristics over time and can actually improve with age, which is why it is sometimes called "winy.")

Green teas are shorter-lived; they are best drunk in the first six months after harvest.

Fresh Tea Is Hard To Find

Most consumers have no idea how old a tea is when they buy it. Indeed, it may take as long as a year for tea to travel from a remote garden to an auction center to a blender's warehouse to the store shelf. (Even in the jet age, most tea is imported by ship.) In the meantime, the essential oils in the tea leaves evaporate, and the flavor gradually disappears.

To keep tea tasting fresh, store the leaves in an airtight container, protected from light. A tin with a tight lid is ideal; it's a good practice to mark it with the date of purchase. Always store tea in a cool, dry place, away from strong-smelling substances such as garlic or spices that can taint its flavor.

CHAPTER 2

TEA HISTORY, CULTURE, AND CUSTOMS

The World of Tea - Tea in China - Tea in Japan
Tea in India - Tea in Ceylon
Tea in the West and Elsewhere - Tea in England
The International Language of Tea

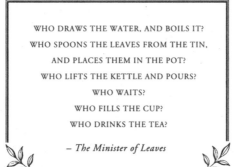

WHO DRAWS THE WATER, AND BOILS IT?

WHO SPOONS THE LEAVES FROM THE TIN,

AND PLACES THEM IN THE POT?

WHO LIFTS THE KETTLE AND POURS?

WHO WAITS?

WHO FILLS THE CUP?

WHO DRINKS THE TEA?

– The Minister of Leaves

The World of Tea

Tea is a universal beverage, consumed in greater quantity world-wide than any other drink except water.

Yet in no two places does "tea" mean exactly the same thing, nor do the customs surrounding it resemble each other. Ask for tea in the British Isles, and you'll be served a black, robust blend, usually of leaves from Ceylon and India; if you take it without milk, you may elicit a raised eyebrow. In China, the same request may well bring you a pot of fine Oolong. In Japan, "tea" means green tea, and green tea only. And only in America will you probably be asked, "Iced or hot?"

Top Ten Tea-Drinking Nations, 1988-1990 per capita consumption	
REPUBLIC OF IRELAND	3.09 kg
UNITED KINGDOM	2.74 kg
TURKEY	2.24 kg
QATAR	2.17 kg
IRAQ	2.14 kg
HONG KONG	1.82 kg
KUWAIT	1.62 kg
NEW ZEALAND	1.58 kg
TUNISIA	1.47 kg
EGYPT	1.38 kg

Canada is twenty-sixth, at 0.53 kg per capita. The United States is twenty-eighth, with 0.34 kg. Figures for China were not available.

1 kg = 2.2 pounds or 440 cups, about 1 1/4 per day, every day of the year.

Tea in China

Tea unquestionably had its genesis in China, but its exact birthdate remains shrouded in myth. Chinese written history is filled with references to tea, which generally date its origin at about 3000 B.C. Tea was initially considered a medicine, gradually evolved into a social beverage, and ultimately became the center of a cultural ritual.

THE EVOLUTION OF TEA IN CHINA

2737 B.C. Legendary accidental discovery of tea by Emperor Shen Nong. While he is boiling water in his garden, a camellia leaf falls from a bush into his pot. Curious, he sips the resulting infusion and declares it has medicinal powers. Earliest recorded references to preparation involve boiling raw, wild-grown leaves in water.

12th century B.C. Next written record of tea indicates that tribal heads include tea in their tributary offerings to King Wen, founder of the Zhou Dynasty.

420-479 A.D. Sung Dynasty Tea is well established as medicine; identified as an aid to digestion and liberator from lethargy. *Preparation:* Raw tea leaves are dried and pounded, compressed into cakes, then broken off into pieces and boiled in water. Results are bitter and unpleasant.

557-589 Chin Dynasty Tea is enjoyed more for its taste than for its effects on health. Sometimes flavored with salt and spices.

589-620 Sui Dynasty Tea propagation becomes more organized and widespread. Tea introduced via Buddhist monks into Japan. Tea bricks emerge as a form of currency used in trade.

620-907 T'ang Dynasty Tea's first "golden age." In 780, the poet LU YU writes the classic *Book of Tea*, an elaborate treatise on every conceivable aspect of growing, preparing, and enjoying tea.

brick tea

Spring tea-harvest festivals become popular, as does the custom of "donating" the very best tea to the emperor (the first recorded tea tax). *Preparation:* Tea bricks are made by steaming raw green leaves, pulverizing them, and reconstituting them as cakes, which are easily sold and transported.

960-1279 Song Dynasty Tea-drinking becomes widespread and is elevated to an art form. Tea rooms and tea houses emerge as social and spiritual gathering places. Special ceramics for tea-preparation and tea-drinking emerge. As northerners become dependent on leaves from the south, they respond by increasing their production of silk to use as trade goods. *Preparation:* Fresh green leaves are dried and powdered, then whipped in a bowl with a whisk. The resulting beverage – bright green, thick, frothy, and potent – is drunk from a bowl. (This style of preparation is still used in the Japanese tea ceremony.)

1368-1644 Ming Dynasty Tea manufacture now involves black, green, and Oolong types. Intense development of special ceramics for tea; Yixing clay pottery and famous blue-and-white designs are introduced. Tea becomes an important trading commodity with countries as far away as Europe. *Preparation:* Round tea pots emerge as preferred vessel for making tea. Leaves replace powder and bricks for the infusion. Small individual cups replace bowls. Tea now drunk continuously throughout the day.

Yixing Teaware. The pottery tradition of Yixing, in China's Jiangsu province, dates back to 2500 B.C. The teapots were first made in the 1500s by the potterer Gong Chun. These small, handmolded and unglazed pots, made of the region's famous purple clay, embody traditional Chinese concepts of beauty and harmony. Their porous interiors absorb a small amount of tea after each infusion, which "seasons" the pot. It is said that if you use a Yixing teapot for many years, you can brew tea simply by pouring plain boiling water into it. Look for the "chop" of the potter on the underside of lid or bottom of pot.

Modern History and Customs. From the early 1600s onward, the story of tea in China is inextricably linked with world history. With rapid advances in global shipping and exploration, tea became China's most important export.

Tea is still bound up with Chinese life and culture. It is served as a beverage, administered as a medicine, and shared as part of a symbolic social ritual.

Tea preferences are diverse and regionally specific, with green tea being considerably more popular than black tea. Some varietals of Chinese green tea are produced in such limited quantities that they are rarely if ever exported.

<hr>

Tea in Japan

Tea arrived in Japan in the early eighth century, brought by Buddhist monks who found its stimulant properties helpful to the practice of meditation. An old legend tells of the Indian monk BODHIDHARMA (or Daruma) who fell asleep while meditating. To ensure this would never happen again, he cut off his eyelids. A tea bush sprang from the spot where they landed, producing a drink that would forever banish fatigue.

Today, the Japanese approach to tea reflects the elaborate ceremonies of the Chinese Song Dynasty, which over time faded in China as they grew in importance in Japan.

The Tea Ceremony. Like no other culture or nation, Japan has elevated the art of preparing and serving tea to a transcendent spiritual philosophy. The Japanese tea ceremony, **Chanoyu**, is a disciplined ritual requiring dedicated study. Yet it also celebrates the simple poetry of life and the communion between host and guest.

tea house

The peaceful tea ceremony has its roots in war. It is said that in the sixteenth century, military leaders would temporarily leave their weapons and differences outside the tea room in hopes of resolving their conflicts over a steaming bowl of *cha*. The elaborate customs enforced an atmosphere of civility and restraint.

In the tea ceremony, every aspect of the experience is meaningful: the design and orientation of the tea room, the path leading through a garden to the tea room, the utensils used to create the tea, the tea itself, the manner in which the host presents the tea. There is a striking emphasis on the simple, economical use of space and objects.

The tea served at the tea ceremony is a bright green powder called **matcha**, made from pulverized tea leaves. It is prepared in a bowl by whisking it together with boiling water. Because what is consumed in the beverage is the leaf itself, a sip of matcha has a relatively high caffeine content.

bamboo whisk

Names to know:

SEN RIKYU, *famous sixteenth-century tea master who elevated the Japanese tea ceremony to "the Way of Tea."*
KAKUZO OKAKURA, *twentieth-century philosopher brought to America in the early 1900s by a group of Boston society women fascinated by Japanese culture and aesthetics. Author of* **The Book of Tea**, *a brief but inspiring treatise on appreciating "the beautiful among the mundane of everyday life."*

Modern Customs. Tea ceremony today is appreciated mostly as an art performed in special tea houses by experienced practitioners. In daily life, most Japanese people drink their tea infused rather than whipped – but still green (usually *bancha*, an "everyday" green tea). It is common for work in a modern office to come to a halt twice a day as the tea cart is rolled through the corridors and "tea break" commences.

Tea in India

Although India is today the greatest tea-producing country in the world, and although wild tea plants are known to grow along the country's northern border, tea-drinking was probably unknown on the subcontinent before the seventeenth century. Then it was a rich person's drink, imported from China and Tibet. The Chinese zealously guarded the secrets of tea cultivation and manufacture.

The British, who thirsted for tea and resented the Chinese monopoly, were struggling to cultivate some stolen Chinese tea plants in their Indian colony. They had a lucky break in the 1820s, when indigenous tea plants were discovered near the Burmese border. Some seeds from those plants eventually made their way to the garden of the Commissioner of Assam. In the 1830s, the commissioner ordered the dense forests of Assam cleared to make way for tea plantings.

Despite plagues of dysentery, yellow fever, and malaria, the British persisted in carving tea gardens out of the mosquito-infested foothills of ASSAM and DARJEELING. From these unpromising beginnings have come some of the world's greatest black teas.

Even so, the tea-drinking style in native India falls short of a connoisseur's standard. In the streets and villages, tea is commonly served boiled with condensed milk and sugar, with cardamom and other spices added to make a grog-like concoction, sometimes called *chai*. The middle and upper classes often drink tea in the British colonial style, with milk and sugar.

Tea in Ceylon

Until the 1880s, very little tea was grown in Ceylon, and that experimentally, using plants from India. Ceylon was famous, instead, for coffee. Then two things happened: a parasite destroyed the island's coffee crop, and THOMAS LIPTON, the British grocery magnate, came to visit.

With land prices bottomed out, Lipton bought four tea plantations and proceeded single-handedly to revolutionize the tea industry. Using the slogan "*DIRECT FROM THE TEA GARDEN TO THE TEA POT*," Lipton made marketing hay out of the lack of a middleman for his product. Four years after his first trip to Ceylon, his plantations and factories employed 10,000 people.

Today, the highlands of Ceylon are planted with world-class tea as well as much average-to-good tea destined for tea bags. The Ceylonese themselves drink very little tea; most of what they produce they export.

※ ═══════════════════════ ❖

Tea in the West and Elsewhere

HOLLAND Dutch mariners brought tea home from Java in about 1610. Most likely these first samples were green Japanese tea, which continued to predominate in Europe for more than a century. The Dutch East India Company quickly monopolized the early tea trade with China and Japan, and introduced the leaf (as well as the ceramic vessels to prepare it in) to other parts of Europe and to Colonial America.

RUSSIA The first Russian czar to sip a cup of tea did so in 1618, when an ambassador delivered a gift from a Mongol prince. After that happy encounter, tea from China made its way to Russia in camel caravans along the arduous overland route. It remained a luxury, available only in the large cities, until the nineteenth century. By then, tea-drinking was the height of French chic, Russians were enamoured of all things French, and tea *à la française* became popular throughout the empire.

The early caravans had a strong influence on Russian tea-drinking customs. To lessen the weight on the camels' backs, the tea leaves were stuffed into cloth sacks rather than heavy wooden chests. During the trek, the leaves absorbed the smoky scent of the evening campfires; this smokiness became a desirable quality in "**Russian Caravan**" tea. Bulky, fragile ceramic cups and pots could not be transported from China, so the Russians devised the *samovar*, an all-in-

Russian samovar

one urn, usually silver or bronze, for preparing and serving tea. A pot on top brewed strong tea, which would be diluted from water in the bottom part of the samovar. A fire in the base kept the water boiling.

The brew was bitter, so drinkers clenched sugar cubes between their teeth and sipped the tea through it.

AFRICA. Tea has been drunk in Egypt since at least the fifteenth century, and today is consumed with a passion. The preferred variety is black, from India or Ceylon, usually in Fanning/Dust form. It is drunk strong and heavily sweetened, and is customarily prepared only by men when it is served to guests.

In MOROCCO, the traditional beverage had always been made from mint leaves alone. In the mid-nineteenth century, British tea merchants introduced green tea into Morocco, where it was enthusiastically blended with the traditional concoction. Moroccan tea – strong, minty, and sugared – is poured in a thin stream from high above the table and served in small glasses accompanied by sweets.

Tea is an important cash crop in many countries of East Africa, notably KENYA. The highest-quality Kenya teas are full-bodied and can rival in quality and character those of Assam. Cameroon, Malawi, Tanzania, Zimbabwe, Rwanda, and South Africa also produce tea – all of it black, some of it very good, much of it destined for tea bags.

THE AMERICAS. Tea may actually have arrived in New Amsterdam (now New York) before it came

THE CLIPPER SHIPS
America's great contribution to the history of tea. After independence from Britain, the fledgling U.S. merchant marine had begun its own tea trade with China. The sailing ships of the late eighteenth and early nineteenth centuries, blunt, full-bodied frigates, proved maddeningly slow. In 1841, a new sailing ship made its debut: knifelike and concave of bow, broad and steep amidships, and slender of stern. The first ship of this design, the clipper "Rainbow," proved so fast that she herself brought back to New York the news of her arrival in Canton, China. She had sailed round-trip in 180 days – faster than any other ship could make the one-way voyage. Within twenty years, the British had clippers of their own, and great races between clipper ships were eagerly followed by newspaper readers on several continents. This Golden Age of clipper ships came to a dramatic end in the 1870s, with the advent of the faster and more economical steamships.

to England. Green tea, the only kind available, became a fashionable drink in the Colonies; it was sometimes flavored with peach leaves and sugar.

By the mid-eighteenth century, the English had supplanted the Dutch, the BRITISH EAST INDIA COMPANY had a monopoly on the tea trade, and tea was the colonies' third-ranking import (behind textiles and manufactured goods). King George III, finding himself in arrears as a result of the French and Indian War, raised the tax the colonists paid on tea. This rankled a number of independence-minded colonists. They responded on December 16, 1773, by dressing up as Mohawk Indians and throwing 340 chests of East India Company tea into Boston Harbor, an event memorialized as the Boston Tea Party. Other "tea parties" followed, and eventually led to the Declaration of Independence. (And, one might add, to a famous national preference for coffee.)

The Invention of Iced Tea. The one form of tea drunk with enthusiasm in the Americas is iced tea. This serendipitous invention was introduced by an Englishman who was running a tea stand at Chicago's Columbian Exposition of 1893. A paralyzing heat wave made fairgoers uninterested in his offerings of hot India tea, so he poured the tea over ice cubes, saved his investment, and changed the tastes of a nation.

Tea in England

Until the late 1600s, all the tea in England was imported from Holland. That changed when the British East India Company – a collective of wealthy British merchants with a royal charter to dominate trade and business by whatever means necessary – persuaded the Crown to forbid all Dutch tea imports. Thus began the world's richest and greatest tea monopoly.

Coffee Houses. By the time tea reached England, coffee – imported from Mexico and Central and South America via Spain – was already established as the hot beverage of choice. The East India Company, spotting an opportunity, promoted tea as an alternative in England's thriving coffeehouses (there were some 2,000 in London by the early 1700s). Whereas coffee had had a reputation as a manly drink, drunk only by men, tea was socially acceptable for both men and women. In 1717, THOMAS TWINING (who went on to found the tea company that still bears his name) opened the first "tea house" to men and women. Very soon, tea replaced ale as the accepted breakfast beverage.

As tea became less expensive and more popular, it also attracted controversy. It was widely (and colorfully) praised, condemned, and misunderstood.

On the pro side was DR. SAMUEL JOHNSON, author of the first English dictionary. He called himself "a hardened and shameless tea-drinker, who has for many years diluted his meals with only the infusion of this fascinating plant; whose kettle has scarcely time to cool; who with tea amuses the evening, with tea solaces the midnight, and with tea welcomes the morning."

On the con side was JOHN WESLEY, the Methodist reformer, who said tea was a waste of money that could better be spent on food. Later, during an illness, Wesley tried tea and became a convert.

Into the Garden. Tea moved out of the coffee house in the middle of the eighteenth century, at least in fair weather, and began to be enjoyed outdoors in **"tea gardens."** In London, famous tea gardens at RANELAGH, MARYLEBONE, and VAUXHALL combined fanciful architecture with arbors, flowered walks, and lavish entertainments such as fireworks and concerts. The gardens attracted royalty, nobility, and sundry social climbers, adding luster to tea's cachet. The phenomenon ran its course over the next century, and the last tea garden closed in the 1850s, a victim, in part, of tea's increasingly popular domestic role.

Afternoon Tea. Afternoon tea was invented in the mid-nineteenth century as a brilliant solution to the stressful British eating habits (heavy breakfast, 8 p.m. supper, not much in between). ANNA, DUCHESS OF BEDFORD, began serving tea, sandwiches, and pastries at four o'clock. (In the twentieth century, the appointed hour became five.)

Within a few years, a formal tea etiquette had been codified, dictating not only the choice of utensils (china or silver, served on fine linens), but also the attire (loose, flowing "tea gowns"), the accompaniments (small sandwiches of cucumber, egg or watercress; scones and berry jam; toast with cinnamon), and the tea itself (Empire-grown India or Ceylon).

OPIUM WARS. By 1800, with the British drinking nearly 5 billion cups of tea a year, the Empire was in financial crisis. The Chinese tea merchants (no tea was yet grown in India) were uninterested in Britain's primary trading good, heavy

broadcloth, so the British had to pay silver for tea. To balance the payments, they turned to a product of their Indian colony: the opium poppy. The British East India Company sold the Indian opium crop in Calcutta, where it was bought by other British firms that sold it – or smuggled it, for it was illegal – in China for silver. By arrangement with the British East India Company, the silver simply stayed in Canton, banked for future tea purchases.

opium poppy pod

The arrangement was tidy for the British but disastrous for the Chinese, millions of whom became opium addicts. In 1839, the Chinese emperor ordered 20,000 chests of opium burned on the beach at Canton. The British responded by declaring war and forcing the legalization of the opium trade. Opium remained a legal item of trade until 1908.

The tidbit-size portions of these aristocratic teas contrasted with the "meat tea" (or, illogically, "high tea") served in working-class homes. **"High tea"** was (and is) a meal consisting of substantial dishes served with tea. It often completely supplanted late-night dinner; workers, after all, had to rise early to keep the wheels of Empire turning.

British Tea-Time Today. The pace of modern life has taken its toll on the twice-daily tea break, once a fixture in British home and work life. Still, afternoon tea remains a cherished, virtually unshakable ritual, and the visitor who drops in at four or five o'clock is almost inevitably offered a **"cuppa."** When tea is served for children, the ritual is known as **"nursery tea"**; children's tea is usually tempered with a good deal of milk and sugar or honey. A **"cream tea"** refers not to the manner of serving the beverage itself but to the substitution of clotted Devonshire cream for butter on scones and other delicacies.

Recipe for Currant Scones: Mix the scone dough, cut, and place on a baking sheet early in the day (up to eight hours ahead). Store, loosely covered with a clean towel, and bake just before serving time. (Makes 1 dozen scones.)

> *2 cups flour, plus flour for dusting*
> *4 teaspoons baking powder*
> *$^{1}/_{2}$ teaspoon salt*
> *$^{1}/_{2}$ cup chilled butter,*
> *plus 2 tablespoons melted butter*
> *$^{3}/_{4}$ cup buttermilk*
> *$^{1}/_{4}$ cup dried currants*

1. Preheat oven to 425° F. In a 3-quart bowl, sift together flour, baking powder, and salt. Dice the $^{1}/_{2}$ cup butter into $^{1}/_{2}$-inch cubes and, using 2 knives or a pastry blender, cut the flour mixture until the mixture resembles small, coarse crumbs.

2. Make a depression in center of flour-butter mixture and gently stir in buttermilk and currants. Mix only until dry ingredients are moistened.

3. Lightly dust a work surface with flour. Place dough and pat into a 1$^{1}/_{2}$-inch-thick rectangle. Cut into squares with a knife. Place on an ungreased baking sheet. Brush with melted butter and bake until light golden brown (about 15 minutes).

4. Serve with butter, honey, or jam and a hot cup of Darjeeling or Assam.

THE INTERNATIONAL LANGUAGE OF TEA
COMMON EXPRESSIONS DERIVED FROM TEA

A NICE OLD CUP OF TEA (British): *A dear person.*

CHALI (Chinese): *Literally, "tea gift," given to a young woman upon her engagement. By extension, the engagement itself. It no longer consists of tea.*

HOCK NIT KEIN CHAINIK (Yiddish): *Literally, "Don't bang a teakettle." Don't make such a big fuss over it; don't bother me.*

LET THE TEA STEEP (German): *Let sleeping dogs lie; forget it. Used in the 1920s.*

NA CHAI (Russian): *Literally, "for the tea." The tip left to a waiter in a restaurant.*

NOT FOR ALL THE TEA IN CHINA: *Not at any price.*

NOT MY CUP OF TEA: *A person, activity, or thing one dislikes. The British used "dish of tea" as far back as the seventeenth century to denote something one enjoyed.*

TEA-LEAF: *In Cockney rhyming slang, a thief.*

TEETOTAL: *To totally abstain from intoxicating drink. Invented by English "teetotaler" Robert Turner in an 1833 speech urging listeners to be "tea drinkers totally."*

TEMPEST IN A TEAPOT: *Much ado about nothing. The Roman usage,* excitare fluctus in simp*luo (to stir up a tempest in a ladle) was already ancient. "A storm in a teacup" was documented in 1872.*

THAT'S ANOTHER CUP OF TEA (British): *That's a horse of a different color; that's another story.*

THE PRICE OF TEA: *As in, "What's that got to do with the price of tea?" Things of real importance.*

WITH NO TEA (Japanese): *Said of a person who is "insusceptible to the serio-comic interests of the personal drama"* (Okakura, The Book of Tea). *Conversely, the person at the mercy of unfettered emotion is said "to have too much tea in him."*

> *Throughout the world, there are only two names for tea: those pronounced "TEA" or "TAY" and those pronounced "CHA" or "CHAI". "Cha" is the Cantonese word for tea; it followed the overland routes on which tea was traded and found its way into languages as far-flung as **Russian, Persian, and Hindi**. "Tea" derives from "tay" in the Amoy dialect spoken in **Fujian** province, across the strait from Taiwan. **The Dutch** learned this version and brought it back to Europe. "Tea" was pronounced "tay" in **English** until about 1712, and is still pronounced that way in **Ireland.***

CHAPTER 3

TEA AND WELL-BEING

The Constituents of Tea:
Caffeine, Polyphenols, and Essential Oils
Summary of Health Benefits of Tea

"It is proper both for Winter and Summer, preserving
in perfect health until extreme old age."
"It maketh the body active and lusty."
"It helpeth the Headache, giddiness, and heaviness thereof."
"It removeth the obstructions of the Spleen."
"It taketh away the difficulty of breathing,
opening obstructions."
"It is good against Tipitude, Distillations,
and cleareth the sight."
"It removeth lassitude, and cleanseth and
purifieth acrid humours, and a hot liver."
"It is good against crudities, strengthening the weakness
of the ventricle or stomach, causing good appetite and
digestion, especially for persons of corpulent body,
and such as are great eaters of flesh."
"It vanquisheth heavy dreams, easeth the frame,
and strengtheneth the memory."
"It prevents and cures agues, surfits, and fevers."
"It strengtheneth the inward parts, and prevents consumption."
"It is good for colds, dropsys and scurvys;
purging the body by sweath, and expelleth infection."

—"THE QUALITIES OF TEA," BROADSIDE PUBLISHED IN ENGLAND C. 1660

The Constituents of Tea

Tea has three principal chemical constituents: **caffeine, polyphenols,** and **essential oils** (also called aromatic or volatile oils).

CAFFEINE is what accounts for tea's reputation as the banisher of fatigue and lifter of spirits. Caffeine is a central nervous system stimulant; it also promotes blood circulation and stimulates the kidneys to produce more urine.

When caffeine was first extracted from tea leaves, in 1827, it was believed to be a substance distinct from the caffeine in coffee, and was given the name "*theine.*" It is now known that they are one and the same.

All types of tea – black, green, and Oolong – contains some caffeine, although the amount varies from type to type.

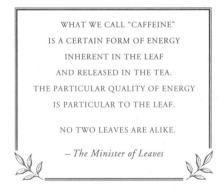

WHAT WE CALL "CAFFEINE"
IS A CERTAIN FORM OF ENERGY
INHERENT IN THE LEAF
AND RELEASED IN THE TEA.
THE PARTICULAR QUALITY OF ENERGY
IS PARTICULAR TO THE LEAF.

NO TWO LEAVES ARE ALIKE.

– *The Minister of Leaves*

CAFFEINE AND TEA: FIVE CONSIDERATIONS

1. The longer the tea leaves have fermented during manufacture, the greater their caffeine content. Green tea, which is unfermented, has one-third the caffeine per cup as black tea, which is fully fermented. Oolong is semi-fermented and has about half as much caffeine as black tea.

2. The shorter the brewing time, the less caffeine ends up in the cup. A four-minute infusion of black tea will produce 40 to 100 milligrams of caffeine, a three-minute infusion only about 20 to 40 milligrams.

"Decaffeinated tea." Appears to be a misguided mid-twentieth century notion based on popularity of "decaf" coffee. Two completely different processes: coffee beans are decaffeinated in their green (unroasted) state, then roasted to bring out their characteristic flavor. Tea leaves must be decaffeinated after fermenting and firing. Result: dull, tasteless tea. Usual remedy: scenting or flavoring (natural or artificial).

Both coffee and tea are usually decaffeinated with ethyl acetate, a natural component of ripe fruits. The non-chemical "Swiss-water" method of decaffeinating coffee beans cannot be applied to processed tea leaves.

Decaffeinated tea is not caffeine-free. It still contains about 3% of its original caffeine content.

3. The smaller the leaf, the stronger the extraction of caffeine. Using comparable amounts and brewing times, a tea bag filled with cut leaf or "dust" will release nearly twice as much caffeine per cup as full-leaf tea.

4. Caffeine's primary effects last about 15 to 45 minutes, depending on an individual's sensitivity.

5. Scientific studies of caffeine to date have been contradictory. There is no conclusive evidence that caffeine causes or exacerbates any specific illness or medical condition.

CAFFEINE PER 6-OZ. CUP, IN MILLIGRAMS	
Espresso (2 oz.)	*60-90 mg*
Drip coffee	*60-180 mg*
Black tea	*25-110 mg*
Oolong tea	*12-55 mg*
Green tea	*8-16 mg*

POLYPHENOLS, once incorrectly called tannins, are responsible for tea's pungency and flavor. Together with the essential oils, these substances also play a role in stimulating the digestive tract. Polyphenols account for about a third of the soluble material in the leaves.

Because of a slight chemical resemblance, tea polyphenols were at one time identified as "tannins" or "tannic acids." Modern chemical analysis has proven the error of this association.

When tea leaves are exposed to oxygen during fermentation, some of their polyphenols are affected and some are not. Those that are affected by oxidation end up producing the color and flavor in tea. Those that remain unoxidized provide tea's astringent, "puckery" quality. Green tea, which is unoxidized, has the most astringency and, conversely, the subtlest color and flavor. Black tea, which undergoes complete fermentation, has the least astringency and deepest color and flavor. Oolong, once again, falls in the middle.

Current research reveals that polyphenols increase the number of white blood cells in the body and boost immunity to disease, inhibits absorption of cholesterol in the digestive tract, and seems to inhibit DNA mutation in rats.

ESSENTIAL OILS contribute significantly to the fragrance of tea and somewhat to its taste. They accumulate in the leaf as it grows and evaporate during and after manufacture. Exposed to strong heat, they will disappear completely, which is why they are also known as "**volatiles.**" Whole-leaf tea retains its oils much longer than crushed leaves, fannings, or tea dust.

Along with polyphenols, the essential oils in tea stimulate peristalsis (contractions of the intestinal tract), which aids digestion.

Green Tea Prevents Lung Cancer?*
In a study, Dr. Fung-lung Chung (American Health Foundation, New York) gave green tea to mice, then exposed them to cancer-causing agent NNK. The mice developed 12.2 lung tumors each – those not given tea developed 22.5 tumors each.

This reveals a possible correlation in humans: cigarette smokers in Japanese tea-producing district have a lower incidence of lung cancer than other Japanese smokers.

Other research shows green tea inhibits formation of stomach and liver tumors in mice.

*International Symposium on the Physiological and Pharmacological Effects of Camellia Sinensis: New York City, March 3-6, 1991

Fluoride In Tea Fights Cavities

Forget what you've heard about apples and carrots being "Nature's toothbrushes." The real cavity-fighter may be tea.

According to the University of California at Berkeley Wellness Letter, *tea is naturally rich in fluoride, the mineral often added to municipal water supplies to prevent tooth decay.*

Most teas sold in the U.S. have 1.32 to 4.18 parts per million (ppm) of fluoride, compared to 0.7 to 1.2 ppm in fluoridated water. And they may have much more. Green "Gunpowder" tea may have as much as 150 ppm.

SUMMARY OF HEALTH BENEFITS OF TEA

GATHERED PRIMARILY FROM RECENT MEDICAL RESEARCH
CONDUCTED IN CHINA AND THE UNITED STATES

Digestion: *Essential oils and polyphenols aid digestion by stimulating peristalsis and the production of digestive juices.*

Cardiovascular system: *Intriguing evidence that Pu-erh, a black tea long famous for its medicinal qualities, reduces blood triglycerides and cholesterol, lowering the incidence of heart attacks. (See page 74 for more on Pu-erh.)*

Teeth: *All teas, but green teas in particular, contain fluoride, a mineral that prevents the development of bacterial plaque leading to tooth decay.*

Cancer: *Polyphenols in green tea have recently been identified as antioxidants and shown to reduce the incidence of skin, lung, stomach, and liver cancers in laboratory animals. Research is preliminary but promising.*

Vitamins: *Some studies show green tea contains significant amounts of vitamin C. Tea also contains small amounts of other vitamins and minerals such as potassium.*

Calories: *Only 4 per cup of tea (black, green, or Oolong).*

Nervous system: *Increases alertness, reduces fatigue, and improves concentration.*

Folk remedies and attributes: *Believed in some cultures to promote longevity. Used in various places as an anti-bacterial agent. Moist leaves used as soothing salves for insect bites and sunburn, as drying agents for fungal infections, and as refreshers for tired eyes.*

CHAPTER 4

A GUIDE TO THE LEAVES

Black Tea Varietals – Black Tea Blends
Scented Black Teas Blended with Fruit
Oolongs – Green Tea Varietals
White Tea

FROM THE MINISTRY OF PROGRESS

*Each varietal of tea usually has several **grades** of*
excellence. These descriptions and tasting notes apply
to the finest grades available to our Republic.
(Some extremely rare "special-grade" Chinese teas
never leave China.) Higher-quality teas lack
bitterness, even after being infused for four minutes
or longer. This advantage carries a price:
special-grade teas often cost as much as 50 times the
price of fourth-grade teas, the most common
grade found in the United States.

Please note, too, that because tea is a natural
product, even the highest grades are subject to
variations in taste depending on weather, soil
conditions, elevation, and freshness.

Black Tea Varietals

ASSAM *(India)* ah-SAHM: Robust, "**malty**" tea with a dark liquor, grown in low-lying Assam region of northeastern India. Often mixed into "**breakfast**" blends; has a heavy character well suited to addition of a little milk. Finer grades are identified by the presence of golden tips, indicating young, desirable leaves. Noteworthy Assam gardens include THOWRA, NUMALIGHUR, PANEERY, BOOTEACHANG, and NUDWA, all recognized for varietals produced according to the orthodox method.

CEYLON *(Ceylon)* say-LAWN *(now Sri Lanka)*: Can denote any tea harvested on the island, from a low-grown leaf cultivated for quantity to a spectacular high-grown tea with a very black leaf that yields a rich golden infusion, lighter and mellower in character than Assam and not as flowery as Darjeeling. Teas grown in the UVA district, between 4,000 and 6,000 feet on the eastern slopes of the island's central mountains, are acclaimed for their special mellowness. Other important districts include DIMBULA and NUWARA, both of which produce teas that lend themselves nicely to blending with fruits and essential oils.

DARJEELING *(India)* dar-JEE-ling: Very fine and rare small-leafed variety from the Darjeeling region in the

Himalayan foothills of NORTHERN INDIA. Noted for its clarity, light but flavorful cup, and complex characteristics. Darjeeling leaves are intentionally broken during manufacture, so you rarely see full leaf even in orthodox-method Darjeelings. The closely planted Darjeeling gardens roll for acres up the mountainsides from 3,000 to 6,000 feet; the higher the elevation, the lighter and more flowery the tea. ("Darjeeling" means "Land of the Thunderbolt.") Leaves produced at different elevations in the same garden often taste distinctly different. Darjeelings are sometimes identified and sold by estate (such as GLENBURN, BLOOMFIELD, NAMRING, or CASTLETON), and by flush – first flush (April/May, light and flowery), second flush (May/June, fruitier and smoother), and autumnal (larger-leafed and "rounder" in taste). Exact timing of the flush depends on when the monsoon rains fall. The Darjeeling aroma is sometimes compared to that of muscat grapes.

Because of their scarcity, Darjeeling teas are only rarely sold unblended. Most store-bought blends include as many as 25 teas from different sources, with perhaps only 50 percent coming from Darjeeling.

KEEMUN *(China)* KEY-min: The most celebrated China black tea, grown in ANHWEI province in east-central China. Fine Keemun has a small, slender, tightly curled, very black-colored leaf and is unique among teas in that it gains rather than loses character with age. Its fragrance is sometimes compared to roses or orchids; also has notes reminiscent of deep chocolate. The infusion is sweet, a tad smoky, and well-bodied. Often enjoyed as a breakfast tea. The absolute finest grade of Keemun, which is not necessarily produced each year because of seasonal variations, is known as **Hao Ya**.

Recipe for Tea Eggs: Hard-boil a dozen eggs in enough plain water to cover them. Crack the shells lightly and put the eggs back in the water. Add in 1 tablespoon Keemun, 1 teaspoon salt, 1 chicken bouillon cube, 1 tablespoon soy sauce and 2 whole star anise. Simmer for at least ¹/₂ hour. Cool and serve.

LAPSANG SOUCHONG *(China)* LAP-sang SOO-shong: Immediately identifiable by its smoky aroma, obtained by withering and drying the leaves over pine fires. Souchongs are grown in China's FUJIAN province. They yield a dark-red infusion that goes especially well with savory dishes.

NILGIRI *(southern India)* nil-GEAR-ee: A **Tamil** word for "**Blue Mountains**," referring to a hilly region at the southernmost tip of INDIA, close to Ceylon. As geography might suggest, high-grown Nilgiris combine the flavor of Ceylon teas with the body of India teas – clean, well-balanced, and slightly lemony.

PU-ERH *(China)* POO-air: An entire class of large-leafed teas from **Yunnan Province** in southwestern China. The more than one hundred pu-erh teas include black, green, Oolong, and brick varieties; all share a folkloric reputation for **medicinal value**. Prized for health benefits, not necessarily taste. Indigestion and diarrhea are two of the maladies pu-erh is purported to cure. "Earthy" in flavor; to enhance the taste, pu-erh is sometimes blended with other teas and flowers such as chrysanthemum.

YUNNAN *(China)* YOU-nahn: Tea grown in a mountainous Chinese province since ancient times. **Yunnan Black** is shipped along with its golden buds, and produces a golden liquor and a rich yet subtle flavor. Aroma is deep and dark, yet retains a floral overtone. Often used in scented tea blends and as a base for fine iced tea.

❧❀❧

Black Tea Blends

ENGLISH BREAKFAST A name created by tea marketers to describe Britain's popular morning blend. Originally indicated a deep, rich mix of Keemun black teas, then any China black tea, later (after the English started growing tea in India and Ceylon) a small-leafed blend of Ceylon and India teas. Today the term may apply to any combination of the above as long as it yields a tea with characteristic medium body and brisk character. Usually drunk with milk.

IRISH BREAKFAST Another marketer's name. More complex, pungent, and substantial than English Breakfast, thanks to the predominance of Assam leaves among other India teas.

RUSSIAN CARAVAN Likely to be any of a number of hearty blends, from China and Formosa Oolongs to unspecified blacks. Lapsang Souchong is often included for its smoky flavor. All Russian Caravan teas have is a striking aroma, supposedly imparted by campfires and camels.

⊰≫✦≪⊱

Flavored and Scented Teas

EARL GREY China black or Darjeeling tea scented with **oil of bergamot**, extracted from a small citrus fruit grown in the Mediterranean region. There are many grades of bergamot oil, some natural, some synthetic. A fine Earl Grey balances and integrates a natural orangey flavor with the tea taste without overwhelming it. Attributed, probably apocryphally, to the British EARL GREY, who visited China in 1830.

JASMINE The jasmine plant was brought to CHINA from PERSIA before the third century A.D., and the intoxicatingly fragrant flowers made their first appearance in tea around the fifth century. The night-blooming flowers are picked in the morning and kept in a cool place till nightfall. Just as they are about to open, they are piled next to heat-dried green tea leaves, which absorb the jasmine fragrance. This process is repeated two or three times for ordinary grades of tea, and up to seven times for very rare and expensive special grades known as **Yin-Hao**. The finest pure jasmine teas have a very clean, balanced, delicate taste. Some jasmine teas are artifically scented with extracts and oils; they have a floral character but lack subtlety. The presence of flowers in the loose tea has no bearing on the quality of the tea; some excellent jasmine teas have no blossoms at all. Folk medicine has it that jasmine tea relieves diarrhea.

SCENTED BLACK TEAS BLENDED WITH FRUIT For centuries, fruit trees have been planted in tea gardens to shade the growing tea bushes. Nature provided the suggestion of combining the two: When breezes blew, the fragrant flowers drifted over the tea leaves and dusted them with pollen and petals. In Assam (India) indigenous mangoes are used; China black tea may be flavored with the juice of the lichee, a sweet-tart fruit native to southern China. Other popular tea-blend fruits include plums, peaches, and cherries. The leaves used in the finest scented teas are often from Ceylon and are generally light-bodied and bright-cupped.

lichee fruit

Oolong Teas

FANCY FORMOSA OOLONG (*Formosa [now Taiwan]*): The finest (and usually most expensive) Oolong, often costing as much as ten times more than other top-grade teas. Infused leaves are rusty brown and very large; leaf-and-bud sets, many with desirable silver tips, can be easily discerned. Highly aromatic, completely lacking in astringency. Fine Taiwan-grown Oolong has the flowery upper register of a top-grade Darjeeling, but a rounder, deeper, fuller cup. Its flavor has been compared to chestnut, honey, and peaches. Finer types lack the dark, tarry, heavy character of lesser grades.

WUYI (*China*) woo-YEE: A large category of Chinese Oolong teas, said to have originated in the WUYI MOUNTAINS along the western border of Fujian province and exported since the eighteenth century. Upon immersion, the crinkled leaves become bright green in their centers and slowly turn red around the edges, a sign of their partial fermentation. Like all Oolongs, it has leaves much larger than those of other varietals.

TI KUAN YIN (Iron Goddess of Mercy) (*China*) tee quawn YIN: The most revered of Chinese Oolongs, it has tightly twisted, shiny dark leaves and a mild taste. It is one of the few teas that can be infused more than once – up to seven times, as lore has it. The tea is known for its digestive properties.

Green Tea Varietals

GUNPOWDER *(China, Formosa):* Said to have been given its name by a British East India Company agent in China who thought it resembled gunpowder. The Chinese call it **"Pearl Tea."** Each leaf is

uninfused leaves

infused leaves

tightly rolled into a pellet that "explodes" when infused with boiling water. Fine gunpowder has a yellow-green liquor and a penetrating, refreshing taste; Formosan gunpowder is notably lighter and sweeter than Chinese. In Morocco, it's used to make mint tea.

HYSON *(China)* HIGH-sun: Not really a varietal but a type of tea made from wild tea trees in west central ZHEJIANG PROVINCE. The leaves are thick and yellow-green and are twisted long and thin during manufacture. The infusion is more full-bodied and pungent than most other green teas. Also called **"Young Hyson."**

DRAGONWELL (**Long Jing, Lung Ching**) *(China):* One of China's most celebrated teas, it has four unique characteristics: light green color, lingering mellow taste, expansive earthy aroma, and long, flat shape. Finest grades still made completely by hand and recognized by their bright and shiny hand-flattened leaf. The tea has a cooling effect welcomed in hot weather.

GEN MAI CHA *(Japan)* ghen my CHA: A Japanese specialty: green sencha tea leaves blended with fire-toasted rice. A hearty tea with a slightly salty, grainy taste that is filling as well as quenching. Finer grades have a natural sweetness to the finish. Sometimes called "**popcorn**" tea – the rice sometimes pops open during shipping.

GU ZHANG MAO JIAN *(China)* goo shong mao chi-ON: Tender, silver-tipped leaves harvested for only ten days each spring on the banks of the Quishui River in the Wuyi Mountains. Infusion has a faint sweetness and unique chestnut character. Although it is a green tea, it is very slightly fermented to give the dry leaves a dark cast. The taste is much smoother than many tra- ditional Chinese green teas and an appealing introduction to green tea for people who have tasted tasted black teas.

GYOKURO *(Japan)* ghee-OH-koo-roe: The finest grade of tea exported from Japan. Flat, sharply pointed leaves like pine needles. Liquor is distinctly green, sweet, and smooth-tasting – a very refined tea for special occasions. Made from first-flush tips plucked from bushes cultivated in deep shade and harvested once a year, in May.

HOJICHA *(Japan)* HO-ji-cha: A large, flat (**unrolled**) leaf that is **oven-roasted** after manufacture to produce an earthy aroma and nutty flavor.

Robust greeting, subtle finish. Low in caffeine; reputed to have restorative qualities.

MATCHA *(Japan)* MA-cha: A powdered leaf that is dissolved in water rather than infused. Yields a bright green beverage ("matcha" means "**liquid jade**" in Japanese). This is the tea traditionally used in Japanese tea ceremony: It is whisked with boiling water in a bowl to create a frothy, nourishing beverage that, like all Japanese teas, is rich in vitamin C. Finest grades are sweet and smooth, with no hint of the bitterness often associated with green teas.

Recipe for Green Tea Ice Cream: Soften 1 pint of vanilla ice cream slightly. Add 1 to 1¹/₂ teaspoons matcha. Beat the mixture until it is well blended. Freeze until firm. Makes 1 pint.

PI LO CHUN *(China)* pee low CHUN: A rare and famous tea whose name means "**Green Snail Spring**"; the hand-rolled leaves do sometimes resemble tiny snails. Its original name, "**Astounding Fragrance**," is also accurate. Planted amid the tea bushes are peach, apricot, and plum trees that are in full bloom when the tender new tea leaves unfold. The shoots absorb the wonderful aromas and pass them on to the lucky person who drinks the tea. Only the bud and a single leaf are plucked, and rolling must be done with great skill to produce the desired snail shape.

White Tea

PAI MU TAN *(China)* pie moo TAHN: Smooth, flowery; yellow-orange liquor with sweet, mellow taste. When infused, the leaves stand upright in the cup. A truly rare tea produced only in China, it is neither rolled nor fermented, only steamed, and is made from buds of a special bush known as "Big White," sometimes blended with buds of the Shui Hsien White Tea plant. Being 100 percent tip, this is the most tender and delicate cup available. Also called "**White Peony.**"

HOW TO READ TEA LEAVES

No one knows where tea-leaf reading began, or what its rules are, or indeed whether it has any rules. It is a practice that is enjoyed in many cultures.

1. BREW A POT OF TEA, but do not use a strainer or infuser basket. A large-leafed variety such as Oolong is most "readable."

2. POUR THE HOT TEA into a classic tea cup with a smooth white interior.

3. DRINK THE TEA, sip by sip. While you do so, reflect on some question you wish the leaves to answer.

4. SWIRL THE TEA CUP when you have finished. Some say to use your non-writing hand, some say to swirl three times in the direction away from yourself.

5. TURN THE CUP UPSIDE DOWN into its saucer.

6. ALLOW THE LEAVES TO TELL THEIR STORY by letting the reader pick up the cup, turn it right-side up, and gaze at the leaves that remain inside.

...Leaves nearest the rim relate to the near future; those farther down describe the more distant future; those at the bottom represent the very distant future.

...The handle of the cup represents the subject of the reading. Its relationship to the position of the leaves indicates one's relationship to the events or persons described by the leaves.

...First impressions are important: they suggest an answer to the question the subject was thinking about while drinking the tea.

...Many leaves in the cup indicate a full, rich life. One leaf stuck on the side foretells the arrival of a stranger.

H E R B S

AN HERB IS A FRIEND.
IT SHOULD BE CHOSEN WISELY
AND ENTERTAINED DISCRIMINATELY.

– The Minister of Leaves

CHAPTER 5

Herbs: A Definition

Herbs - Herbal Beverages: "Infusions" or "Teas"
How Herbal Tea Blends Developed
Growing Herbs - Wildcrafted Herbs
How To Make Herbal Infusions
What To Look for in Herbal Infusions

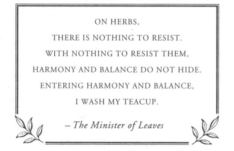

ON HERBS,
THERE IS NOTHING TO RESIST.
WITH NOTHING TO RESIST THEM,
HARMONY AND BALANCE DO NOT HIDE.
ENTERING HARMONY AND BALANCE,
I WASH MY TEACUP.

– The Minister of Leaves

Herbs

Any introduction to herbs must begin with this riddle: What is an herb?

A classical definition is "**plants that lack woody stems and whose leaves, stems, and flowers have aromatic or medicinal properties.**" Yet some flowers (for example, saffron) are called **spices**, not herbs. And the definition of "herb" is frequently stretched to include **roots** (for example, ginseng and licorice), **bulbs** (garlic), **succulents** (aloe), and certain "**woody**" trees (birch and white willow, whose bark was used in traditional medicines).

So here is our own highly subjective definition: HERBS ARE PLANTS THAT SERVE HUMAN BEINGS FOR THEIR ABILITY TO LIFT OUR SPIRITS, SEASON OUR FOOD, DYE OUR FABRICS, HEAL OUR AILMENTS, AND MEND OUR WOUNDS.

Of course, not all herbs are so congenial. Nature's harvest includes many forms of poison, from mildly sedative to dramatically fatal. Hemlock, henbane, mandrake, and belladonna are but a few of the "**witches' herbs**" known through the centuries for their power to paralyze and kill. The humblest plants often are the most benign, while the showiest are sometimes the most dangerous.

Herbal Infusions (Teas)

According to the strict constructionists, "TEA" applies only to beverages made from the leaves of the *Camellia sinensis* plant. Beverages made from herbs, they insist, are properly called "INFUSIONS." In fact, the two terms are often interchanged in casual use, leading to considerable confusion, at least in the United States.

We side with the loose constructionists, and use "herbal infusion" and "herb tea" to mean the same thing.

There are several categories of herbal preparations.

INFUSIONS, called *tisanes* in French, are beverages made by steeping dried or fresh plant parts in water that has come to the boil.

DECOCTIONS are primarily for medicinal purposes and are made by boiling the plant parts in water until the liquid is reduced. The water is then strained into a cup or teapot.

EXTRACTS are concentrated preparations made by evaporating the liquid (water, alcohol, or ether) in which a plant has been boiled. Extracts are generally not used for "teas."

TINCTURES are potent medicinal extracts of plants in alcohol or a mixture of alcohol and water. The herbs steep for as long as two weeks, and the solution is shaken daily. Tinctures are normally added to water when taken for medicinal purposes.

Hot or iced herbal infusions are often desired as caffeine-free alternatives to tea, coffee, or cocoa. However, several herbs – among them maté, guaraná, cola nuts, ephedra, and gotu kola – in fact contain caffeine or other stimulants. Other herbal brews may produce welcome or unwelcome sedative, laxative, or diuretic effects.

How Herbal Teas Developed

Over the centuries, through countless experiments, people have found ways to derive the most pleasure and benefit from herbs. Usually that meant blending them. Although some people prefer a single herb's flavor alone, most enjoy the synergistic effect of several in a blend.

Simples and blends. That said, the first herbal teas were almost certainly made from one herb at a time. A single herb was known as a simple; the process of experimenting with it was called simpling. Simpling is still the best way to appreciate the flavors and effects of each herb and to understand how blending enhances them.

Some herbs, such as chamomile or peppermint, are frequently enjoyed in their unblended form. Others, such as valerian and goldenseal, have a bitter taste best disguised by the addition of other herbs and spices. Certain combinations blend so happily that they are classics: linden blossoms and peppermint, for instance, or rose hips and hibiscus.

hibiscus

Growing Herbs

Every common herb, and many not-so-common ones, grew wild at one time in the past. Some still do. (And some only seem to, as anyone who has tried to clear out a mint patch from a garden will attest.)

Today, the herbs used in infusions are usually grown in one of three ways: from a windowsill or backyard garden, from a commercial plot, or collected in the wild ("**wildcrafted**").

No two herbs demand exactly the same growing conditions or cultivation techniques, which is why many commercial growers specialize in a particular species.

Wildcrafted Herbs

Many important herbs are still wildcrafted, or gathered from wild habitats all over the world. The flowers of the linden tree (*Tilia cordata*), traditionally used in a fever-reducing tea, are picked one by one by villagers standing on tall wooden ladders along European country lanes. In North America, ginseng was wildcrafted to virtual extinction in the nineteenth and early twentieth centuries; it is now cultivated commercially. However, the tradition of wildcrafting in the United States lives on in the Ozark Mountains and other rural areas.

Some herbalists say wildcrafted herbs are the most potent, medicinally speaking, and the purest because they have been taken from their natural habitat. On the other hand, they don't always taste as good as their cultivated cousins, which have been selected for their flavor components.

How To Make Herbal Infusions

It is as easy to prepare a satisfying herbal infusion as it is to prepare a delicious cup of tea (*Camellia sinensis*). That is:

BOIL WATER.

INFUSE HERBS.

DRINK INFUSION.

Attention to a few details can help distinguish a merely pleasant cup from a truly exceptional one.

Use fresh cold water. The purer and better-tasting the water, the more satisfying the results. Experiment with tap, filtered, and bottled waters if you are interested in finding the best alternative.

Fill a kettle with water and bring it to a rolling boil.

Use full-leaf herbs. Leaves and flowers release their essences most fully when they are preserved in their entirety. Pulverized herbs in tea bags can't compare: when the herbs are very finely cut, their essential oils (which are responsible for fragrance and taste) evaporate quickly. Infusers (see below) are easy to use and a far superior alternative to tea bags.

Infuser, cup, and teapot. Herbs need space and good water circulation to unfold and release their essences into the water. For infusing, choose a bamboo, plastic, or wire mesh basket that can be dipped into a single cup. Or try a ceramic infusion basket that fits into the top of a mug or within a teapot. Avoid perforated stainless-steel tea balls; they don't allow sufficient water flow or leaf expansion.

Next, select a ceramic or glass tea cup and teapot. Metal pots can impart a metallic flavor to the herbs, and may sometimes even leach undesirable minerals into the infusion. Warm the teapot or cup by swirling some steaming-hot water in it, and then pour it out.

How much herb? One rounded teaspoon of dried herb per cup – one-and-a-half to two grams – is usually sufficient. Some blends are naturally stronger than others, so experiment.

How long to steep? About five minutes, more or less depending on your preference. When first sampling a new herb or blend, taste it at intervals to determine the desired strength.

Remove the herbs or strain off the liquid when the tea reaches the desired strength. Dispose of them in your flower garden or compost pile; they make a fine mulch and fertilizer.

To make iced herb tea, use two rounded teaspoons of dried herbs or three of fresh. Pour over ice cubes. The melting ice will dilute the strong tea.

You may also make a regular-strength hot infusion and chill it in the refrigerator. This method takes a little longer, but some people claim it yields a better-tasting iced infusion.

What To Look for in Herbal Infusions

Here is where herbal "teas" really differ from *Camellia sinensis* teas. There is no standard language for evaluating herbal infusions, because every herb, every blend, and every cup is likely to be different from the last. A few guidelines may be helpful – but, as usual, let your own taste be your guide.

BODY. The body of the tea is the base that carries the flavor notes. A well-formulated herbal tea has a strong body that lends a deep and full dimension to the beverage. Flat, weak, and watery teas are undesirable.

COLOR. Depending on the dominant herb, infusions may range from light yellow-green (desirable in chamomile tea) to golden (characteristic of teas made with cinnamon or cardamon) to deep brown (as with chicory and carob teas) to bright red (as with hibiscus). In general, the color should appeal to the eye and associate pleasantly with the flavor, body, and fragrance of the beverage.

FLAVOR. A well-blended herbal tea reveals a full complement of flavors with high, middle, and top notes. (The irresistible comparison is to fine perfume.) No single flavor should overwhelm the others. With practice, you may be able to distinguish three or four flavor notes – **green, flowery, fruity, spicy**, and so on.

Some commercially available herbal blends are enhanced by essential oils or concentrated juices and others are created from chemically isolated flavors derived from natural or artificial substances. For example, infusions made from strawberry and raspberry leaves are sure to disappoint anyone expecting "strawberry" and "raspberry" flavors – they have none of the sweetness of the flavor of the fruit. Essential oils and concentrates from fruits, herbs, and spices, as well as highly engineered derivatives created in a laboratory, are often added to enhance their flavor and satisfy the expectations of the sipper.

"NATURAL" VS. "ARTIFICIAL"*

NATURAL FLAVOR(ING): *The essential oil or other extract of a spice, fruit, vegetable, edible yeast, herb, bark, bud, root, leaf, meat, seafood, poultry, eggs, or dairy product, whose significant function in food is flavoring rather than nutritional.*

ARTIFICIAL FLAVOR(ING): *Any substance used to impart flavor to food that is not derived from the above list.*

*Source of definitions: U.S. Food and Drug Administration

CHAPTER 6

Herbs in Myth, History, and Lore

Herbs in China - Ayurvedic Traditions
Herbs in Egypt - De Materia Medica
Nuns, Witches, and Herbalists
Native American Herbalism
Herbs in the Modern World

mandrake root

Beginnings

Who knows how humans first came to know which herbs were good to eat and which had healing properties? Maybe our ancestors were gifted with phenomenal powers of intuition. Maybe they got ideas from watching grazing animals. Most likely, they slogged along through centuries of trial and error.

We do know that by the time the **Chinese**, the **Indians**, and the **Egyptians** made the first written records of such things, 3,000 to 4,000 years ago, herbal medicine was already very ancient and quite sophisticated.

Herbals

So sophisticated, in fact, that all three cultures left confident, detailed descriptions of the herbs they knew and used. So did later cultures, including the **Romans**, the **British**, and the **Americans**. These books, sometimes organized like encyclopedias, are known as herbals.

Herbals not only tell how people of a certain place and time used herbs for cooking, medicine, and cosmetics, they also revealed much about the culture's world view. Because they tended to be written for laypeople, they often reflected folk beliefs as well as the scientific dogma of the day.

It's tempting to smile at these works. They take themselves terribly seriously, and many of their theories now seem farfetched or even dangerous.

But some of our contemporary scientific "knowledge" about herbs may someday appear just as ludicrous when new discoveries are made.

The First Herbal: *Pen Tsao Ching*. The *Pen Tsao Ching* is real, but the story of its origins is mythical.

The Yellow Emperor, SHEN NONG, who lived for about a thousand years, was a remarkable personage indeed. For one, he had a transparent abdomen, through which he could observe the workings of his digestive system. Even more amazing, he was semi-immortal, capable of dying and being reborn. These two attributes served him well as the father of herbal medicine (and, not coincidentally, the discoverer of *Camellia sinensis*). By tasting a great number of herbs and observing their effects, he learned which herbs were beneficial and which were harmful or even fatal. Eventually, alas, he died permanently, but not before passing on his knowledge to grateful mortals.

Shen Nong's legacy, said to have been written about 2700 B.C., is the *Pen Tsao Ching*, or *The Classic of Herbs*. It lists more than 300 herbal remedies made from a wide variety of plants, including ephedra, rhubarb, and opium poppy. In time, other herbalists added to this body of knowledge by writing their own herbals. To date, some 400 herbals, describing 5,000 plant-based medicines, have been written in Chinese. Not surprising when you consider that China has some 30,000 flowering plant species – the most diverse flora of any non-tropical nation. North America has only about 18,000 flowering plant species.

The *Pen Tsao Ching* also set forth the basic principles of Chinese medicine, which involving balancing the forces of YIN and YANG (complementary types of energy), heat and coolness, energy and inertia, dryness and moistness, and other pairs of opposites. These principles and practices have had an amazingly long lifespan. Herbs, acupuncture (stimulation of energy channels with fine needles), diet, and exercise, all described in the *Pen Tsao Ching*, are still commonly used in Chinese medical treatments.

> *BALANCING THE QI. The animating force of Chinese medicine is known as QI (pronounced "**chee**"), which Westerners sometimes liken to "**energy field**." The purpose of Chinese medicine is to balance the forces within the human organism, which the Chinese regard as a MICROCOSM OF NATURE. Instead of viewing doctors as mechanics, as Westerners often do, the Chinese view doctors as **gardeners** – pruning, fertilizing, and planting to create a harmonious, thriving whole.*

The Herbal of the Hindu Gods. Forty-five hundred years ago, according to Indian legend, the Hindu gods instructed the first human physicians in AYURVEDA, *the science of life.* Their lessons were compiled in ancient texts called **Vedas.** One of those texts, the Rig Veda, contains formulas for medicines combining 67 herbs, including ginger, cinnamon, senna, serpentwood (the source of the modern anti-asthmatic medicine reserpine), and garlic (with which ancient Ayurvedic healers claimed to have successfully treated leprosy).

THE LEGEND OF PUNARVASU ATREYA. A disciple of Punarvasu Atreya, founder of India's first medical school, studied for seven years with the master. At the end of that time, he asked Atreya when he would complete his training. "Go out into the countryside," said Atreya, "and bring back all the plants that have no medical use." The student eagerly set out, but returned emptyhanded after several days. "I could not find a single plant without healing power," he told his teacher sadly. Satisfied, Atreya told him: "Go! You are now ready to be a physician."

The Secrets of the Pharaohs. The herbal that would end up having the greatest influence on the Western world was written in Egypt, probably around 1500 B.C. In 1874 a German Egyptologist discovered it – a 65-foot-long roll of papyrus that describes surgical procedures, internal medicine, and herbal remedies. Among the 800 medicinal herbs it lists are anise, cassia, cardamon, thyme, and **garlic** – a special favorite of the Egyptians, who believed it strengthened the body and prevented disease.

garlic bulb

Modern science tends to agree with the Egyptians about garlic. LOUIS PASTEUR observed garlic's antibacterial effects back in 1858, and in the second half of the twentieth century more than 1,000 scientific papers have been published on the uses of garlic to fight infection, reduce blood pressure, and lower blood cholesterol.

Latin Lore: *De Materia Medica.* Europe's first true herbal was written around the turn of the first millennium A.D. by one DIOSCORDES, a Greek born in Turkey who served in the Roman Emperor Nero's army. *De Materia Medica*, as the herbal was called, was influenced by Egyptian traditions but represented a step backward. Dioscordes did discuss about 500 plants, but so vaguely and briefly that it is hard today to know exactly which ones he was talking about.

Nevertheless, largely for lack of anything else, *De Materia Medica* influenced herbal medicine for 1,500 years. Well into the sixteenth century, it was still widely quoted and relied on.

THE LANGUAGE OF HERBS

DERIVATIONS AND DEFINITIONS
OF SOME WORDS OFTEN SEEN IN HERBALS.

ANGELICA: *Once believed to have "angelic," or heavenly, powers. It is one of very few herbs nearly always referred to by its Latin, rather than a common, name.*

CHAMOMILE: *From the Greek words meaning "ground apple," a reference to the herb's fragrance and flavor.*

DIGITALIS: *The Latin name for foxglove means "of the finger," because the plant's flowers are finger-shaped.*

HYSSOP: *This common name comes to us via Latin and Greek from the Hebrew* esob, *"holy herb," which is mentioned in the Old Testament. However, the Biblical plant was probably some other herb — maybe a species of marjoram.*

OFFICINALIS: *As the second half of a Latin name (e.g.,* Salvia officinalis*), indicates that the herb was once an "official" medicine.*

TUSSILAGO: *From the Latin* tussis, *"cough." This herb, commonly called coltsfoot or coughwort, was once widely prescribed to coughing and wheezing patients.*

VALERIAN: *May come from the Latin* valere, *meaning "to be strong or healthy." Or it may be named in honor of Valerius, an early herbalist.*

WORT: *The Anglo-Saxon word for "plant," part of such common herb names as St. John's Wort, mugwort, soapwort, and milkwort.*

Nuns, Witches, and Herbalists

The fall of Rome in the fifth century A.D. ushered in the Dark Ages, aptly named as far as herbal learning goes. Scientific inquiry, such as it had been, came to a halt. Non-Christian learning was suspect. Herbalism survived as an artifact of the ancient world, cloistered in Catholic monasteries where nuns and monks copied the ancient texts and grew "**physic gardens**" containing plants that could be used in teas and remedies.

Folk herbalists, meanwhile, did what folk herbalists had always done: they treated diseases with plants as best they could. Illiteracy was rampant, so the oral tradition prevailed, but occasionally a sympathetic cleric would be moved to write down some local superstitions, usually without comment or criticism. WALAHFRID STRABO, a monk who lived in what is now SWITZERLAND during the ninth century, wrote such a collection in verse form. Of sage he wrote, "It holds the place of honor, is of good scent, and virtues for many ills" – some of which, he claimed, included palsy, indigestion, and toothache. He also suggested an antidote to poisonous aconite: "a dose of wholesome horehound." That would be the same innocuous horehound familiar to us in throat lozenges.

In the eleventh century, a German Benedictine abbess, HILDEGARD OF BINGEN, claimed to be inspired by divine visions to compile her herbal formulas into a book. A jumble of folk medicine, Catholic mysticism, and practical herbal experience, *Hildegard's Medicine* is among the very few collections of the "**old wives' tales**" told by "**wise women**" who served as the doctors of the day.

By 1300, similar "wise women" – a literal meaning of "**witch**" – were being burned at the stake throughout Europe. As practitioners of herbal medicine, they were regarded by the Church as confederates of the Devil; healing preparations were condemned as sinister poisons and aphrodisiacs.

The Doctrine of Signatures. The Renaissance was a golden age of "**official**" herbal medicine. Hundreds of herbals were published; some actually contained useful information. Most mixed religion, superstition, astrology, and convoluted metaphysical doctrines with a bit of botanical lore.

The most peculiar dogma of the age was the Doctrine of Signatures. This theory argued that the Creator had marked each plant with a "**sign**" of its benefits to man. Yellow plants, such as **marigold** and **saffron**, were certainly meant to treat jaundice, which makes the skin yellow. Plants whose leaves resembled the liver would heal liver disease. And plants like **mandrake**, which looked like the human form, were believed to be God's gift to the entire body.

mandrake root

Trade Roots. Such fanciful notions as the Doctrine of Signatures were about to meet their demise. Travel and exploration proved their downfall.

THE CRUSADES of the eleventh through thirteenth centuries did more than introduce a new kind of religious war; they also introduced Europeans to the comparatively sophisticated medical practices of the Middle East. In the Arab and Persian worlds, there had been no Dark Ages. Greek and Roman medicine had been preserved, studied, and further developed. In addition, the Near Eastern countries had their own indigenous herbs, exotic and promising to European eyes.

Later journeys encouraged further exchange of ideas and medicines. The voyages to the Americas brought back a wealth of new plants such as **cinchona**, the Peruvian bark that yields the malaria drug quinine. Traveling in the opposite direction, sixteenth-century Dutch explorers brought **sage** to the Chinese, who became so enamoured of sage tea that they gladly traded three pounds of their own tea for one pound of dried sage.

Sage tea was also drunk by eighteenth-century American patriots boycotting English tea imports. It was recommended by American doctors as late as the 1920s as a gargle for sore throats.

sage

Names to know:

NICHOLAS CULPEPER, *Puritan herbalist and astrology buff. Wrote the extraordinarily influential (and highly unreliable)* Complete Herbal and English Physician *in 1652; never since out of print. First translation of Latin medical knowledge into English; also touted folk remedies of English country people.*

MRS. MAUDE GRIEVE, *Twentieth-century British herbalist. Author of* A Modern Herbal *(1931), subtitled* "The Medicinal, Culinary, Cosmetic and Economic Properties, Cultivation, and Folk-Lore of Herbs, Grasses, Fungi, Shrubs & Trees with All Their Modern Scientific Uses." *In two volumes; includes detailed descriptions of more than 800 plants.*

Aconite. *Some species of Aconite were well known to the ancients as deadly poisons. It was said to be the invention of Hecate from the foam of Cerberus, and it was a species of Aconite that entered into the poison which the old men of the island of Ceos were condemned to drink when they became infirmed and no longer of use to the State. Aconite is also supposed to have been the poison that formed the cup which Medea prepared for Theseus.*

From Mrs. M. Grieve, *A Modern Herbal,* 1971, Dover Publications

Herbs in the Americas

Unlike the Egyptians and the Chinese, the Indians of North and South America did not write herbals. Nevertheless, by the time of the European conquests, they had clearly honed their skills. Spanish observers in the sixteenth century noted that the NAHUAS of Mexico had a well-developed medical system. And COTTON MATHER, the Puritan minister and doctor, wrote in the late seventeenth century that North American Indian healers produced "many cures that are truly stupendous."

Among the herbs the indigenous Americans introduced to Europeans are some plants still used medicinally in one form or another: **black cohosh** for menstrual pain and difficult childbirth, **echinacea** for colds and infections, **slippery elm** for sore throats. The CHEROKEES used **goldenseal** to treat arrow wounds; the AZTECS used **wild yams** in poultices for boils; the SHOSHONES made a tea from **lobelia leaves** to induce vomiting.

lobelia

Herbs in the Modern World

Travelers exploring the world today will find a well-established herbal tradition in virtually every culture they visit. In "developing" countries, as much as three-quarters of the population may be treated primarily with herbs by local practitioners. In Europe, where doctors often prescribe herbal extracts and homeopathic remedies, herbal medicines are sold in pharmacies (or **"chemists' shops"**) alongside "modern" pharmaceuticals. And in the United States, herbalism is being embraced by people as various as New Age seekers and elderly arthritis sufferers.

Meanwhile, concern about environmental catastrophe has motivated some people to try to save unique, endangered pools of herbal knowledge. In the **Amazon**, plant species are disappearing rapidly as the rain forest is destroyed; older herbalists there are finding few apprentices. **Ethnobotanists** from universities have been trying to record some of this tribal knowledge, but the task is vast and already much has been lost.

*HERBS AND HOMEOPATHY. Homeopathy is a paradox. It uses minute doses of plant extracts to cure those disease symptoms that the same plant produces in large doses. First formulated in 1810 by a devoutly religious German physician, SAMUEL HAHNEMANN, homeopathy differed dramatically from the prevailing medical methods, which depended on huge doses of powerful substances such as mercury and poisonous herbs, as well as radical surgery and bloodletting. One of the first homeopathic experiments involved **quinine**, which caused fevers in healthy people and cured people with malaria. Homeopathy derives from the Law of Similars — "like cures like." It is widely practiced in many countries, including England, France, Greece, India, and Sri Lanka.*

CHAPTER 7

HERBS AND WELL-BEING

Herbs and Medicine
The Poppy Yields Its Secret - Active Principles
Whole Herbs Are Safer
Modern Medicines Derived from Plants
The Case of Ginseng - The Case of Ginger

foxglove

Herbs and Medicine

People have used herbs as medicine for as long as there have been people who got sick. According to archaeological evidence, humans in MESOPOTAMIA (now Iraq) used **yarrow, marsh mallow**, and other healing herbs some 6,000 years ago. More than 100 of our most valuable drugs – among them **digitalis, quinine**, and the ubiquitous **aspirin** – are derived from common plants used since antiquity in the healing arts.

Healers in the past were hardly infallible. They often prescribed a single herb for dozens of wildly unrelated conditions – say, fever, digestive problems, kidney stones, and delayed menstruation (all "known" to be cured by **chamomile** in seventeenth-century England). Some herbs went through fashions of being used to treat one thing in one century, another in the next. (In nineteenth-century America, some physicians prescribed chamomile for malaria and typhus.) Once in a while, the herbs must have done the trick. (Or maybe it was simply that the boiled water used for herbal infusions was much safer than unboiled, untreated water from the local creek or well.)

And sometimes an herb acquired a consistent reputation, in diverse cultures and many eras, for successfully treating one malady in particular. In cases such as this, even modern science became interested.

The Poppy Yields Its Secret

Until the early 1800s, most medicines were crude plant preparations administered orally – leaves, flowers, roots, and barks, or teas made from them. Doses were difficult to standardize, and patients had no way of knowing whether a particular plant preparation was in fact what it was supposed to be.

Active Principles. All that changed dramatically in 1803, when a German pharmacist isolated **morphine** from opium, the milky juice of the opium poppy. For the first time, physicians could give exact doses of the medicinally potent part of the plant – its active principle. Throughout the nineteenth century, scientists hunted for other active principles. By 1870 they had isolated caffeine from coffee, quinine from cinchona, cocaine from coca, and many other drugs from their plant sources.

For all its benefits, this approach had serious drawbacks. There's a lot more to a plant than its active principle (itself quite complicated). Opium, for example, contains twenty-two chemical compounds; morphine is the dominant one, but not the only active principle.

Whole Herbs Are Safer. Whole herbs or herbal infusions tend to be milder in effect than the drugs refined from them, and they are generally safer. Digitalis leaf, which was a standard remedy for "dropsy" (congestive heart failure) until the

1920s, contains a built-in safeguard: if you take too much, you get sick to your stomach. When **digitoxin** was extracted from digitalis, doctors stopped using the whole leaf. Now patients who overdose don't simply get queasy – they develop dangerous heart irregularities. It seems the more isolated the components of the plant one uses, the more dangerous the potential side effects.

WE SING GINSENG. Name an ailment, and it is likely that ginseng has been touted as its cure. The knobby root has been prescribed at various times for colds, coughs, depression, impotence, menstrual problems, arthritis, memory improvement, diabetes, high blood cholesterol, and cancer. It has also been assailed as a hoax and a fraud.

The truth probably lies somewhere in between. The ancient Chinese called ginseng *jen shen,* meaning *"***man root,***"* because to some eyes it resembled a human form. If it looked like a man, the theory went, it must be beneficial for the ills of man. Its most popular use has always been as a whole-body tonic; the legendary emperor Shen Nong claimed that "continuous use leads to longevity." It enjoys an unsubstantiated reputation as an aphrodisiac, perhaps also because of its appearance. Ginseng's fame spread far beyond Asia in the eighteenth century, and it was glorified with a Latin name, *Panax,* that means **panacea,** or cure-all.

There are actually three kinds of ginseng: **Chinese** (which is the same as **Korean**), **American**, and **Siberian**. The Siberian plant is not a true Panax but rather a prickly shrub *(Eleutherococus senticosus)* belonging to the same botanical family as *Panax*. American ginseng was first discovered by a French explorer in 1704 and enjoyed a boom throughout the Colonial period. It is now a commercial crop in Wisconsin.

Since the 1960s, most of the research into ginseng has been done in Russia, China, and the United States. One Russian study reported that ginseng stimulates the immune system (workers who took it had fewer sick days), an American study reported that it eliminated chronic herpes sores (they came back when treatment ceased), and both Russian and Chinese researchers have claimed some success in treating cancer patients with ginseng-based remedies.

Modern Medicines Derived from Plants

ASPIRIN. Salicin, the base of the compound of acetylsalicylic acid, which is aspirin, is naturally present in the bark of the **white willow tree** (*Salix alba*), found in many regions of the world. In fact, every traditional herbal medicine, from the Chinese to the African Hottentots to the Native North Americans, has used white willow bark and other salicin-containing plants, usually in the form of tea, for the same maladies we now treat with aspirin:

pain, fever, and inflammation. In the first half of the nineteenth century, European chemists extracted first salicin from meadowsweet *(Filipendula ulmaria)* which was thought to be a member of the *Spiraea* genus for which aspirin eventually was named. It took the work of several more chemists to develop the synthesized aspirin compound. Aspirin continues to be one of the most widely used (some might say overused) nonprescription drugs available.

COLCHICINE. The ancient Egyptians treated gout with the bulbs and seeds of the **autumn crocus** (*Colchicum autumnale*), a deceptively lovely plant that carries poison in every part. Slaves in ancient Greece, knowing of its deadliness, chewed tiny bits of the bulbs to wangle sick leave. Today we have less toxic methods of malingering but still no more effective treatment for gout. Colchicine is isolated from the plant and given intravenously or in tablet form. *Even this treatment can have serious side effects; under no circumstances should anyone experiment with autumn crocus on his or her own.*

DIGITOXIN. The tall, beautiful **foxglove plant**, which grows wild along roadsides and at the edges of woods, has been cultivated for herbal medicines used for various conditions for centuries. In the 1700s, a British physician "discovered" that foxglove tea was being used as a folk treatment for dropsy, or congestive heart failure. His account of his discovery and the subsequent isolation of digi-

toxin from the plant led to its widespread medical use. Digitoxin, 1,000 times stronger than powdered digitalis leaves, helps reduce blood pressure in the veins while stimulating the heart's contractions. *Both digitoxin and the foxglove plant itself are too toxic to be used without medical supervision.*

EPHEDRINE. Ephedra has been used for more than 5,000 years in China, where it is called *ma huang*. The entire plant contains ephedrine, a potent stimulant and relaxant of bronchial smooth tissue; it's used as a decongestant and asthma drug. Ephedrine was isolated from ephedra by Chinese researchers in the early twentieth century; it is the "**-fed**" in over-the-counter decongestants with that suffix. An American species, *E. nevadensis*, contains much smaller amounts of ephedrine.

QUININE. Tea made from the powdered bark of the **cinchona tree** was a traditional malaria remedy among Peruvian Indians. Spanish conquerors took the medicine back with them to Europe in the seventeenth century, when malaria was a global scourge. It thus became the first **specific** in Western medicine – a particular medicine for a particular disease. Quinine, isolated from the bark in the mid-nineteenth century, was used both as a preventive and a treatment for malaria well into the twentieth century, when synthetic malaria drugs were developed. In recent years, the malaria parasite has become resistant to synthetic drugs, and quinine is once again returning into favor.

RESERPINE. This drug for high blood pressure is isolated from the root of the **serpentwood tree** (*Rauwolfia serpentina*). The plant is native to the rain forests of India, and is mentioned as a gentle sedative in a medical handbook written around 1000 B.C. In the 1940s, serpentwood's active principle was isolated and Indian physicians began prescribing it for hypertension. *The regular use of reserpine has a documented side effect of manic depression – a side effect possibly buffered in the whole root by counterbalancing compounds.*

ROSY PERIWINKLE. Native to Madagascar, the rosy periwinkle (*Catharanthus roseus*) has had a folk reputation as a treatment for diabetes. It is now reported to have a promising effect on white blood cells in cancer cases. Few wild specimens of the plant can still be found in their original habitat.

Ginger Rules the Waves. Centuries ago, Chinese sailors chewed ginger to prevent seasickness. Now research confirms they were doing the right thing. A 1985 study published in the respected British medical journal Lancet *found better results with ginger powder than with the over-the-counter motion sickness drug Dramamine; the stout-hearted volunteers were subjected to computerized rocking chairs. Ginger tea, ginger powder, candied ginger, and ginger ale all seem to work about the same but – make sure the ginger ale is made with real ginger and not an artificial substitute.*

CHAPTER 8

A GUIDE TO
THE BOTANICALS

Berry Leaves - Fermented Herbs
Flowers - Fruits
Lemon-Flavored Herbs - Mints
Other Aromatic Herbs
Sleep-Inducing Herbs - Sweet Herbs
Tonic Herbs
Rainforest Herbs and Spices
Roasted Grains and Roots - Spices

spearmint

This index of botanicals – edible herbs, spices, and roots – is selective for a reason: Our focus is herbs used in teas rather than herbs used in medicines, cosmetics, or other products. That is why the plants have been categorized here according to the parts most frequently used for teas, or the type of tea for which they are most frequently used. Within each category, the herbs or spices are listed alphabetically.

NOTE:

No matter how long its medicinal history or favorable its reviews, no herb is free from unwanted side effects in some people. Reactions may range from hay fever-like symptoms to poisoning and even death from highly toxic plants. Never experiment with herbs picked from the wild; when trying a new herbal infusion, sample a little bit at a time until you are satisfied it agrees with you.

A GLOSSARY OF COMMONLY USED HERBAL CATEGORIES

ADAPTOGENS *Herbs believed to strengthen and enhance the immune system and balance internal bodily functions.* Ginseng, echinacea, pau d'arco.

ALTERATIVES *Substances believed to gradually improve health and vitality, once known as "blood cleansers."* Sarsaparilla, echinacea, burdock, garlic.

ANALGESICS *Herbs that can relieve pain. Also called "anodynes," particularly when applied externally.* Arnica (external use only), lady's slipper, skullcap, white willow.

ANTIDIARRHEALS *Substances that may combat diarrhea.* Blackberry, cowberry, peppermint, wild strawberry.

ANTISPASMODICS *Herbs that may ease spasms or cramps in muscles or internal organs.* Ginger, hawthorn, chamomile, valerian.

ASTRINGENTS *Substances that can tighten or shrink tissues and are sometimes used to stop bleeding or close skin pores.* Eucalpytus, witch hazel, agrimony, betony.

CARMINATIVES *Substances that reduce flatulence.* Angelica, cayenne pepper, caraway, cardamon, ginger, fennel, peppermint.

CATHARTICS *Herbs that can promote movement of the bowels. Laxatives are mild cathartics; purgatives are strong ones.* Dandelion, licorice, senna, barberry.

DIURETICS *Herbs that can stimulate the secretion and elimination of urine.* Parsley, uva-ursi, marsh mallow, dandelion.

NERVINES *Substances that can stimulate or relax the nervous system.* Hops, ginseng, chamomile.

SEDATIVES *Herbs considered calming to the nervous system. Less-potent herbs are sometimes called calmatives.* Valerian, passion flower, skullcap, catnip.

STIMULANTS *Substances thought to increase the physiological functions of the body. Stimulants work more quickly than tonics.* Hyssop, cayenne pepper, feverfew.

TONICS *Substances believed to strengthen specific organs or the entire body.* Rosemary, echinacea, ginseng, goldenseal.

VULNERARIES *Herbal preparations applied externally to aid in healing wounds.* Aloe, marsh mallow, comfrey, calendula (pot marigold).

Re: Plant Names. Common or "country" names of herbs are picturesque but not very helpful – Quaker bonnet, hoodwort, helmet flower, mad-dog weed, and skullcap are all names for the same plant. Luckily, one two-word Latin name – Scutellaria lateriflora *– cuts through the confusion.*

The scientific naming system was devised in the eighteenth century, when Latin was the lingua franca *of scholars. The first word denotes the* **genus***, the second word the* **species***. When a plant has several different species, the genus name may be abbreviated to a single letter – as, for example, with* Echinacea angustifolia *and* E. purpurea.

Berry Leaves

BLACKBERRY *(Rubus fruticosus, R. villosus)* Neutral flavor with an astringent note – nothing at all like blackberry fruit. Astringency comes from tannin content of leaves and root, which mimics that of black tea. Not palatable unless blended with other herbs and spices. Both species (EUROPEAN and NORTH AMERICAN) used for many centuries to cure a number of disorders, including diarrhea, dysentery, mouth sores, and gum inflammations.

RASPBERRY *(Rubus idaeus)* Astringent and rather unpleasant-tasting; needs other herbs to make it palatable. Often found in special teas for pregnancy because of traditional reputation for preventing miscarriage and easing child-birth. Twentieth-century British researchers found that a constituent of the leaf, fragarine, is capable of both stimulating and relaxing uterine muscle tissue.

STRAWBERRY *(Fragaria vesca, F. americana)* Milder, not as astringent as the other berries  yet still "puckery" enough to substitute for black tea in blends. Originally wildcrafted in EASTERN EUROPE, now harvested from commercially grown fields as a secondary product to the fruit.

Fermented Herbs

MATÉ *(Ilex paraguariensis)* An acquired taste – infusion is bitter, astringent, and unpleasant at first, like black coffee. Leaves sold either green or roasted; the latter have a pleasant toasty flavor. Rich in vitamin C, tannins, and caffeine – a six-ounce cup contains between 50 and 100 milligrams of caffeine, about the same as a cup of coffee and about twice as much as a cup of black tea. Native to BRAZIL, PARAGUAY, and ARGENTINA, where it's made into a thick paste and drunk from a hollowed-out gourd ("**maté**" in Spanish) through a tube ("**bombilla**") with a filter at one end to screen out the sediment. Guarani Indians of Paraguay used it as a stimulant and scurvy preventive in their all-meat diet. Today cultivated extensively in Argentina, where maté drinking is a social event that can last several hours.

bombilla

ROOIBOSCH *(Aspalathus linearis)* Round, "full" taste without bitterness, sweetness, or astringency (very low tannin content; no caffeine). Combines well with milk. Used to lend body and color to herb tea blends. Native only to the southwestern Cape region of SOUTH AFRICA; traditionally used for tea by the Khoisan, Bushmen, and Hottentots. Name is Dutch for "**red bush**." The fermentation process, which requires a high degree of skill, involves bruising and moisturizing the needle-like leaves.

Flowers

CHAMOMILE (*Matricaria chamomilla* or *Anthemis nobilis*) Fragrance is sweet and apple-like; taste is floral with a bitter afternote. One of the most popular tea herbs in the world; drunk as a single herb tea and also blended with lemon-flavored herbs, linden flowers, other flowers. The two plants known as chamomile come from unrelated species, yet have similar daisy-like flowers and long histories in folk medicine. Used to treat everything from malaria (in ancient EGYPT) to indigestion (in medieval GERMANY). Contemporary German pharmaceutical companies produce chamomile extracts for a wide range of conditions, including skin injuries and insomnia.

Recipe for Chamomile Cookies. These small cakes are especially good with a hot cup of chamomile tea. Makes 2 dozen.

> *1 stick butter or margarine, softened*
> *1 cup sifted all-purpose flour*
> *²/₃ cup brown sugar*
> *2 medium egg yolks*
> *grated rind of 2 lemons*
> *1 ¹/₂ teaspoons crushed dried chamomile flowers*

Cut the butter into the flour until the mixture resembles crumbs. Add the rest of the ingredients and, using floured hands, knead the mixture. Cover and chill for 30 minutes. Heat oven to 325ºF. Roll the dough into 1-inch balls. Place on a pan and flatten with the bottom of a fork. Bake for 12-15 minutes.

HIBISCUS *(Hibiscus sabdariffa)* Fresh, tangy; contains small quantities of citric acid and vitamin C; rich in calcium, niacin, riboflavin, iron. Usually found in blends with fruits and spices; popular both hot and iced. Turns tea a bright-red color. Part used in tea: **calyces** (leaf-like enclosures of unopened flower buds). Not to be confused with ornamental hibiscus *(H. rosa-sinensis)*, it's a bushy shrub sometimes grown for its jute-like fiber. Originally native from INDIA to MALAYSIA; naturalized in AFRICA, THE WEST INDIES, CENTRAL AMERICA, THAILAND, and CHINA.

LAVENDER *(Lavandula officinalis, L. angustifolia,* and other species) Tastes the way it smells: sharp, perfumy, aromatic. Too strong to be drunk without blending; in blends, provides a distinct top spike of flavor and a refreshing quality. Only unfaded, deep-blue flowers should be used; they turn tea a purplish-blue color. May have originated in INDIA, but quickly made its way to the MEDITERRANEAN; still an important commercial crop in the south of FRANCE. "Lavender" comes from Latin *lavare,* "**to wash**"; may have been used to scent baths and linens in Roman times.

LINDEN BLOSSOMS *(Tilia cordata)* Deliciously sweet, flower-nectar flavor. Blossoms picked by hand by harvesters standing on tall ladders to reach tops of tall linden trees; it takes many blossoms to yield a single pound. Because of high labor costs, no longer offered in most commercial U.S. tea blends, but is very popular in Europe. Linden tea reputed to soothe nervous complaints, lower blood pressure, aid digestion.

ORANGE BLOSSOMS *(Citrus aurantium)* Flowery orange-nectar flavor; very popular in herbal tea blends. Petals are collected from the ground after fertilization; quality varies. According to MRS. MAUDE GRIEVE, author of *A Modern Herbal* (1931), an infusion of the flowers alone was traditionally drunk by Europeans as a mild nervous stimulant. Other sources claim it's a sedative.

ROSE PETALS *(Rosa* spp.*)* Mildly astringent; delicate floral nectar flavor. Originally cultivated by the cultures occupying the ancient NEAR EAST; spread to ancient GREECE and ITALY. **Tea rose** (*R. indica*) named for resemblance of its fragrance to black tea.

Fruits

LEMON PEEL AND JUICE *(Citrus limonum)* Bright, tangy-tart flavor. Lemon juice in concentrate is a natural flavor enhancer for herbal teas. High in vitamin C; famous for its role in defeating "sailor's scourge," **scurvy**. Wild lemon tree probably originated in NORTHERN INDIA; brought to Europe by Arab traders.

ORANGE PEEL *(Citrus aurantium)* Stronger flavor than orange blossoms – rich, full, signifying presence of orange oil. Used for centuries to flavor food and tea; source of "orange" in most orange-spice tea combinations. First introduced to the West by the Arabs; now cultivated throughout the world in the temperate zone, most notably SPAIN, ISRAEL, and CALIFORNIA.

ROSEHIPS *(Rosa canina)* Tart, fruity flavor; turn an infusion reddish-brown. Typically mixed with 20 to 30 percent hibiscus as the flavors and colors are complementary. Vitamin C content higher than that of oranges, ounce for ounce; also high in vitamins A, B, E, and K, as well as organic acids and pectins that make rosehips mildly laxative and diuretic. Rosehips are the fruit of the **dog rose** *(R. canina)*, a wild variety.

Lemon-Flavored Herbs

LEMON BALM *(Melissa officinalis)* Mellow, flowery, soothing lemon flavor. Popular in France in teas; known there as *Thé de France*. Blends well with chamomile. Main flavoring ingredient in Benedictine and Chartreuse liqueurs. Named by the Greeks for the bees that hover around it, but not to be confused with "**bee balm.**" The great eleventh-century Arab scholar AVICENNA wrote, "Balm causeth the mind and heart to become merry." In fact, lemon balm can be a mild sedative and digestive aid.

LEMON GRASS *(Andropogon* spp.) Invigorating citronelle lemon note that hits high in the mouth. Popular culinary addition in THAILAND and VIETNAM; also found growing in CENTRAL AMERICA. During the 1970s, became an addition to herb tea blends in the United States. European tea drinkers were introduced to it shortly thereafter.

LEMON THYME *(Thymus serpullum,* var. *citriodorus)* Fragrant round thyme flavor with a lemon tone. Blends well with ginger, mints. A variety of wild thyme; **thymol**, its active constituent, has strong antiseptic properties and can be in digestive and respiratory complaints. MOROCCO and HUNGARY produce lemon thyme for the European market; grown organically in the PACIFIC NORTHWEST.

LEMON VERBENA *(Aloysia triphylla;* also called *Lippia citriodora)* Deep, refreshing, perfumy lemon flavor. Popular tea herb native to the AMERICAS; brought to EUROPE by the Spanish conquerors of Chile and Argentina. Reputed to have digestive properties similar to the mints and lemon balm.

Mints

BERGAMOT MINT *(Mentha piperita, var. citrata)* Unique perfumy flavor compared both to lavender and to Bergamot oranges (the flavoring ingredient in **Earl Grey** tea). Sometimes called **eau de Cologne mint** or **orange mint**; said to have the same digestive properties attributed to the other members of the mint family.

PEPPERMINT *(Mentha piperita)* Cool menthol flavor with pleasant sharpness; slightly astringent. Used alone or in blends, hot or iced. Often enjoyed after meals: essential oil of peppermint, **menthol**, stimulates the flow of bile to the stomach and helps relieve gas pains.

SPEARMINT *(Mentha spicata)* Milder and sweeter than peppermint; more widely used in cooking. Commonly known as a toothpaste or chewing gum flavor. Originally native to the MEDITERRANEAN region; now grown throughout the world.

Recipe for Mint-Cherry Granite. *Make an infusion with ³/₄ cup of mint leaves and 2 cups of boiling water. Steep 5 minutes and strain. Combine liquid with 7 cups of pitted cherries, 1 cup of sugar, and 2 tablespoons of lemon juice in a blender. Blend well. Strain and freeze in a flat pan. When well frozen, scrape with a spoon into glasses. Makes 10 servings.*

Other Aromatic Herbs Used in Teas

ANISE HYSSOP *(Agastache foeniculum, A. rugosa)* Light, sweet, anise-scented flavor; flowers and leaves are used in herb tea blends. Grows wild in NORTH AMERICA from Ontario to the midwest of the United States; originally cultivated for its beautiful blue flowering spikes. Chippewa and  Cheyenne traditionally drank anise hyssop tea for respiratory problems and chest pains. Related Chinese giant hyssop grows wild in China, Korea, Japan, and Taiwan. According to traditional Chinese medicine, it "opens the stomach"; used in Chinese medicinal formulas as a carminative, to stop vomiting, for colds and flu, and for angina pains.

ROSEMARY *(Rosemarinus officinalis)* Fresh, strongly aromatic, wholly characteristic fragrance and flavor. Used in herbal tea blends. Chinese doctors traditionally mixed it with ginger to treat headache, indigestion, insomnia, and malaria. Name, meaning **"dew of the sea,"** comes from its deep-blue flowers, which grow best along seacoasts.

SAGE *(Salvia officinalis)* Intense camphor flavor. Enjoyable mixed with honey and lemon. Found growing wild in the MEDITERRANEAN; widely naturalized. Name comes from Latin *salvare,* **"to heal or save."** Has been credited at one time or another as a virtual panacea and prescribed for headaches, hemorrhoids, depression, palsy, and a litany of other maladies. Many folk traditions included a belief that sage would lengthen a person's life if taken regularly.

WINTERGREEN *(Gaultheria procumbens)* Cool, wispy, minty flavor. Wildcrafted for herbal tea industry; adds a fresh note to blends. Native to NORTH AMERICAN evergreen forests and traditionally prized by various Native American tribes for its ability to ease the pain and inflammation of rheumatism. Active ingredient, **methyl salicylate,** has pain-relieving properties similar to aspirin. Most over-the-counter external analgesics (also toothpastes, cough drops, chewing gum) are based on the synthetic version of methyl salicylate.

Sleep-inducing Herbs

HOPS *(Humulus lupulus)* Bitter, unpleasant; must be blended with other ingredients to be palatable. Native Americans used hops flowers for a sedative tea. Because of bitterness, used in very small quantities in commercial herb teas. Acts as a preservative and flavoring agent in beer; causes familiar drowsiness after "one too many"; transforms sweet ale into bitter beer. Native to both EUROPE and NORTH AMERICA. One of the few crop plant species that bear male and

female flowers on different plants; only female flowers used in brewing and in medicine. European folk belief: sleeping on pillow stuffed with crushed dried hops will cure insomnia.

PASSION FLOWER *(Passiflora incarnata)* Mild, straw-like flavor, attributable to abundance of stem used along with leaf. Flowers and fruiting tops are soothing and can be mildly sedative in an infusion. Wildcrafted in southeastern UNITED STATES; state flower of Tennessee. Discovered by a Spanish doctor in the PERUVIAN ANDES who regarded it as a sign that God approved of the conquest, and named it for the **Passion of the Cross.**

SKULLCAP *(Scutellari lateriflora)* Green, alfalfa-like flavor. Often included in relaxing herb tea blends. Whole plant is harvested; cultivated plants are more pleasant-tasting than wildcrafted ones. Found throughout EUROPE and ASIA, but only the species native to the southern part of the UNITED STATES is known for its sedative qualities.

Native American tribes in that region used skullcap as a sedative and to bring on menstrual periods. Recent studies in Europe and Russia have supported skullcap's effectiveness as a tranquilizer and sedative, attributed to **flavonoid glycosides** in the volatile oil.

TILIA *(Terstronemia* spp.) Deep, dark flavor completely unlike that of botanically unrelated *Tilia europea,* the linden flower for which it is sometimes substituted in herb tea blends. Pods are used. Native to MEXICO; used as a sedative among Mexican Indians, but no studies have confirmed its effectiveness. Tilia pods are also used in potpourri because of their attractive star shape.

VALERIAN *(Valeriana officinalis)* Bitter, disagreeable odor and taste. Must be blended with other herbs or flavoring agents to be palatable. Different species of *Valeriana* grow throughout EUROPE and NORTHERN ASIA; European species harvested commercially for its roots. Centuries-old folk tranquilizer and sleep aid; modern studies indicate that active ingredient is indeed a tranquilizer. During World War II, used in England as a treatment for "air-raid nerves." Pharmaceutical drug Valium, also a tranquilizer, unrelated to valerian other than linguistically.

Sweet Herbs

ANISE *(Pimpinella anisum)* Sweet and aromatic. Famous flavoring agent of beverages from digestive teas to **Turkish arrack** to **Greek ouzo** to **French anisette.** Member of the *Umbelliferae* family that also includes dill, fennel, caraway, angelica and cumin; cultivated in MEDITERRANEAN region since the time of the Pharaohs. Essential oil identical to that of cheaper, stronger-flavored star anise, which has largely replaced aniseed oil commercially. All the Umbelliferaes are esteemed for their carminative (gas-dispelling) properties. Anise is used in cough medicines and lozenges for its reputed bronchial benefits.

CAROB *(Ceratonial siliqua)* Pods abound in natural sugars yet are low in calories and fat, high in B vitamins and calcium. *Also see section on roasted grains.*

LICORICE *(Glycyrrhiza glabra)* Sweet, somewhat "rooty." Often used in teas to mask the taste of bitter herbs, especially the tonic herbs, and to add its own characteristic flavor. **Glycyrrhizin**, one of its primary constituents, is 50 times sweeter than sugar. **Native Americans** in the eastern UNITED STATES used licorice tea as a cough remedy and laxative. Licorice also appears in early EGYPTIAN papyri; a bundle of licorice sticks was found in

King Tut's tomb. Soothing, coating properties make licorice effective in cough, sore throat, and stomach ulcer preparations. If taken in sufficient quantities, can cause potentially dangerous water-retention. Up to 90 percent of imported licorice used by tobacco industry to flavor cigarettes. Licorice candy today contains no licorice at all, but is flavored with similar-tasting anise oil.

STEVIA *(Stevia rebaudiana)* STEE-vya. Intensely sweet; almost unpalatable at full strength. Excellent blended with bitter or bland-tasting herbs. Contains no calories yet is 300 times sweeter than cane sugar. Used for more than 400 years by the Guarani Indians of PARAGUAY to sweeten food and teas. Contemporary Japanese have done extensive research on stevia and use stevia extracts to flavor many foods and diet beverages.

Tonic Herbs

ECHINACEA *(Echinacea angustifolia,*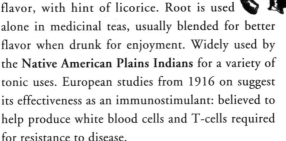
E. purpurea) Eh-kin-AY-sha. Caramel root flavor, with hint of licorice. Root is used alone in medicinal teas, usually blended for better flavor when drunk for enjoyment. Widely used by the **Native American Plains Indians** for a variety of tonic uses. European studies from 1916 on suggest its effectiveness as an immunostimulant: believed to help produce white blood cells and T-cells required for resistance to disease.

ELEUTHERO GINSENG *(Eleutherococus senticosus)* Eh-LOO-ther-row. Pleasantly neutral bark flavor; produces a light yellow tea. Dried, pulverized roots are used for tea as well as for medicines. Native to CHINESE and RUSSIAN SIBERIA, eleuthero is sometimes marketed as Siberian ginseng, but this can be misleading: more familiar *Panax* ginseng also grown in Siberia. Has been shown to prolong the endurance of athletes, ameliorate nervous disorders, and improve various chronic conditions.

GINSENG *(Panax ginseng, P. quinquefolius)* JIN-seng.   Strong, rooty, unpleasant taste; strong odor. In tea, usually blended with other herbs or flavoring agents for palatability. Native to CHINA and NORTH AMERICA; known as **Chinese or Korean ginseng** and used in Asia since ancient times. Classic Chinese herbal *Pen Tsao Ching* says ginseng enlightens the mind, increases wisdom, gives longevity to the user. Latin name, *Panax*, means "**panacea.**" Prescribed in traditional Chinese medicine to improve chronic conditions, strengthen body to cope with stress, restore vitality, and boost immune system.

SARSAPARILLA *(Smilax ornata, S.officinalis)* Sass-pa-RILL-ah.   Mild, "**root beer**" flavor. Often added to tea blends to improve or balance taste. The root of a woody vine, sarsaparilla is harvested from wild plants in the tropical forests of MEXICO, JAMAICA, and CENTRAL AMERICA. Once famed as a tonic cure for syphilis and skin disorders; base of many nineteenth-century tonics in U.S.

SCHIZANDRA *(Schizandra sinensis)* Shi-ZAN-dra. Fruity and sour; used in tea blends as a counterpoint to sweet herbs. The dried red berries are used. In CHINA, known as "**five flavors**"– various parts of the fruit have sweet, sour, pungent, bitter, and salty tastes, encompassing all five elements central to Chinese medicine. The berries are used as a tonic in various chronic conditions.

Rainforest Herbs and Spices

ALLSPICE *(Pimenta officinalis, P. dioica)* Combines the flavors of cloves, cinnamon, nutmeg, and pepper. Berries are used in cooking; leaves  are used for tea – they produce a full-bodied infusion with a flavor similar to that of the berries. Native to CENTRAL AMERICA, MEXICO, and the WEST INDIES. Berries, which resemble black peppercorns ("**pimientas**" in Spanish), were brought to Europe by the Spaniards in the sixteenth century.

PAU D'ARCO *(Tabebuia impetiginosa* or *hepaphylla.)* Pow DARK-oh. Pleasant, full-bodied flavor; tea is dark red. Can be drunk by itself or blended. Inner bark or heartwood of the tree is used. Careful harvesting techniques permit gathering inner bark without killing tree. *Tabebuia* species grow in rainforests from MEXICO to ARGENTINA, and many Indian tribes claim various medicinal uses for it. Studies performed at the University of Munich show that low dosages of pau d'arco have immunostimulating properties similar to those of echinacea.

VANILLA *(Vanilla planifolia)* Sweet, full, heady, complex flavor. Dried beans of an orchid, or their liquid extract, used to flavor herbal tea blends. The only member of the orchid family to be used for food; discovered by **Mexican Indians** before the Spanish conquest. Cultivated in many tropical parts of the world; vanilla from MEXICO and MADAGASCAR considered the finest. Vanilla production very labor-intensive: Flowers must be hand-pollinated and each bean handled some 400 times during the curing process. No medicinal claims.

YERBA SANTA ACUYO *(Piper sanctum)* Unique spicy anise flavor. Large, heart-shaped leaves (twelve to sixteen inches across) used in tea and cooking. Related to pepper and many other food plants. Found growing by waterways in the middle altitudes of the rainforests in SOUTHERN MEXICO. A staple of Central American cuisine since before the Spanish invasion; popularly included there in tamales, salsas, fish and egg dishes, and digestive and bronchial teas.

Roasted Grains and Roots.

BARLEY *(Hordeum vulgare)* Adds a dark, grainy flavor and color to herb teas. Barley malt, made from dried germinated grain, often used in tea for its high sugar content. Roasted barley also a popular substitute for coffee. Cultivated since Neolithic times; esteemed by ancient EGYPTIANS and GREEKS for nutritive qualities. Beer made from fermented barley was one of the earliest alcoholic beverages.

CAROB PODS *(Ceratonial siliiqua)* Sweet, round, roasted flavor without bitterness. Roasted, powdered pods are cut into small pieces to flavor herbal blends; good complements include cinnamon and the mints. Often substituted for chocolate because of comparable color and flavor. Tall evergreen tree native to SOUTHWESTERN EUROPE and WESTERN ASIA. Derives name from "**carat**": seeds once used as a counterweight in measuring gold. Traditional medicinal uses include diarrhea remedy.

CHICORY ROOT *(Cichorium intybus)* Pleasantly bitter "**roasted**" flavor; adds dark color to tea. Often added to coffee; reputed to mellow the caffeine effects. Cultivated as far back as EGYPTIAN times; common sight along NORTH AMERICAN byways. Cultivated much more extensively in EUROPE than in United States. Bitter greens are eaten in salads; Belgian endive and radicchio are varieties of *Chichorium.*

Spices

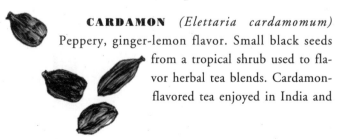

CARDAMON *(Elettaria cardamomum)* Peppery, ginger-lemon flavor. Small black seeds from a tropical shrub used to flavor herbal tea blends. Cardamon-flavored tea enjoyed in India and parts of Africa; cardamon-flavored coffee favored in the MIDDLE EAST and NORTH AFRICA. One of first spices brought to EGYPT along trade routes from eastern INDIA. Grows only in rainforests with at least 150 inches of annual rainfall; exported primarily from MALABAR, MYSORE, and CEYLON. Seeds are encased in a green pod that keeps flavors fresh and strong; once pods are opened, much flavor and aroma are lost. Seeds can be chewed to sweeten the breath.

CASSIA *(Cinnamomum cassia)* Like **cinnamon**, but hotter and spicier. Sold interchangeably on the commercial market with true cinnamon; preferred in tea blends for its stronger flavor. Most powdered "cinnamon" on the market is actually cassia or a combination of cassia and cinnamon. As with cinnamon, the bark (removed from young shoots of the mature evergreen tree) is used. Indigenous to CHINA; written about in the *Pen Tsao Ching* (circa 2700 B.C.). Arab traders brought it to MEDITERRANEAN during early days of the spice trade. Used in traditional Chinese medicine as a warming stimulant; reputed to enhance vitality and stimulate all body functions.

CINNAMON *(Cinnamomum zeylanicum)*
Sweet, pungent. Used to flavor herbal and black teas. Spice comes from inner bark, which curls naturally into quills or sticks. Native to CEYLON; now cultivated widely in the tropics. Grows in forests up to 1,000 meters in elevation, needs constant rainfall.

Contemporary Japanese research suggests cinnamon may help reduce blood pressure.

CLOVES *(Syzygium aromaticum* or  *Eugenia aromatica)* Bitter, pungent. Spice is derived from the **calyx** (unopened flower seed pod), beaten from the tree before seed has matured. Used in tea and cooking. Clove tea reputed to cure nausea. Originated in the MOLUCCAS, five small islands in the southern Pacific also known as the **Spice Islands** because of their botanical riches.

GINGER *(Zingiber officinale)* Invigorating, pungent flavor with a "bite." Chopped or powdered root used in cooking; chopped root makes a fine tea – boil for five to ten minutes, strain, add honey and lemon. Native to SOUTHEAST ASIA, where the Chinese discovered it and began employing it for medicine and spice. Taken to Europe on the spice routes; reached New World in sixteenth century. Best-quality ginger now comes from CARIBBEAN islands. In Chinese medicine, used as internal warming stimulant that works specifially on stomach and chest.

MACE AND NUTMEG *(Myristica fragrans)* Aromatic, sweet; mace is subtler than nutmeg. Both used to flavor cooking and teas. Derived from the same plant: mace is the dried brittle yellow covering of the nutmeg seed. Cultivated

in tropical rainforests of the EAST AND WEST INDIES, COSTA RICA, INDIA, CEYLON AND BRAZIL.

PEPPERCORNS *(Piper nigrum)* Hot, piquant. Traditionally used in Indian spice tea formulas. Pepper berries collected unripe and sundried to produce black pepper; or ripe and with hulls removed to produce less-piquant white pepper. (Pink peppercorns come from *Schinus terebinthifolius* tree from South America and are less piquant.) Native to INDIAN RAINFORESTS; mentioned in Sanskrit texts from fourth century B.C. Quest for pepper drove the spice trade, made many Arabs and Venetians rich. In early European history, peppercorns often used as currency.

STAR ANISE *(Illicum verum)* Sharp, spicy flavor, deeper than that of aromatic anise seeds. Dutch began using it to flavor tea in seventeenth century, imitating the Chinese custom. Fruit is star-shaped, with glossy brown seed pods contained in the points of the star. Originated in SOUTHERN CHINA and NORTHERN VIETNAM. Star anise's essential oil later became a flavor replacement for the more expensive aniseed oil in liqueurs such as anisette. Star anise is used in Chinese medicine as carminative, stimulant, and diuretic.

A TOAST TO THE GRACE OF THE POT,

READY AT ALL TIMES

TO GIVE UP ITS EMPTINESS

FOR THE TEA.

—The Minister of Leaves

FOR FURTHER EDIFICATION AND ENJOYMENT

The Book of Tea (Paris: Flammarion, 1992). Sumptuously illustrated "tea-table" book, translated into English by Deke Dusinberre and with a preface by the British writer Anthony Burgess. Evocative descriptions of early life in the tea gardens of India and Ceylon, excellent cultural history of tea-drinking, and useful color photographs of full-leaf tea varietals.

Blofeld, John. *The Chinese Art of Tea* (Boston: Shambhala, 1985). A veteran China traveler and scholar, Blofeld gives an informed yet highly personal account of emperors and monks, poets and potters, all linked in the great stream of tea. Includes descriptions of many rare and legendary Chinese teas.

Castleman, Michael. *The Healing Herbs: The Ultimate Guide to the Curative Power of Nature's Medicines* (Emmaus, Pennsylvania: Rodale Press, 1991). Useful, accessibly written encyclopedia of herbs that emphasizes medicinal value but also discusses herbs for enjoyment.

Chow, Kit, and Ione Kramer. *All the Tea in China* (San Francisco: China Books and Periodicals

Inc., 1990). China-born and Hong Kong-educated Kit Chow began his research into tea as a quest to improve his personal health. His studies yielded a trove of fascinating information on the arts and customs of tea as well as contemporary scientific information.

Goodwin, Jason. *A Time for Tea: Travels through China and India in Search of Tea.* (New York: Alfred A. Knopf, 1991). A young Englishman's quixotic contemporary journey to the lands of tea. A travelogue that is also a lively history and a smart, funny commentary on the tea trade then and now.

Grieve, Maude. *A Modern Herbal.* (New York: Dover Publications, Inc., 1982) A twentieth-century version of the Renaissance herbal, originally published in 1931 and still invaluable as a source of scientific and superstitious lore. In two volumes.

McCormick, Malachi. *A Decent Cup of Tea* (New York: Clarkson N. Potter, Inc., 1991) A charming little book by an expatriated Irishman with some refreshingly brisk opinions about his beverage of choice.

Okakura, Kakuzo. *The Book of Tea* (New York: Dover Publications, 1964 Also a nice teeny-tiny new edition from Shambhala, 1993) The modern classic written by a Japanese scholar who charmed turn-of-the-century New England and became the curator of East Asian Art at the Boston Museum of Fine Arts. An elegant appreciation of the letter and the spirit of Japanese tea ceremony.

Pratt, James Norwood. *The Tea Lover's Treasury* (San Francisco: 101 Productions, Cole Group, 1982). An authoritative introduction to tea, written in a resoundingly original voice. Packed with fact, legend, and anecdotes.

Ukers, William H. *All About Tea* (Whitestone, New York: Tea & Coffee Trade Journal Co., 1935). Two volumes. Out of print and hard to find. A classic and in many ways still the definitive source of information about tea history, culture, literature, and trade. Filled with fascinating illustrations and black-and-white photos.

INDEX

ACKNOWLEDGEMENTS

Editor

Nancy Friedman

Research

Nancy Friedman

Bill Rosenzweig

Gina Amador

Carolyn MacDougall

Design and Illustrations

Gina Amador

This book was prepared under the auspices of:

Bill Rosenzweig

MINISTER OF PROGRESS

Bob Lally

MINISTER OF THE INTERIOR

Carolyn MacDougall

MINISTER OF HERBS

Special thanks to The Minister of Leaves and The Minister of Enchantment, Suzy Schuman, Don Roberts, Jane McCabe, Joe Simrany, Ron and Pam Phipps, Michael Spillane, Brian Writer, Esther Wanning for her invaluable editing assistance, and the Cole Group.

ILLUSTRATION CREDITS

Jacket, pp. 11, 83 Patricia Ziegler; jacket, The Republic of Tea; pp. 23, 24, 48 William H. Ukers, *All About Tea* (The Tea and Coffee Trade Journal, 1935); pp. 11, 14, 16, 17, 20, 21, 22, 25, 26, 30, 33, 39, 40, 45, 46, 52, 57, 71, 77, 78, 79, 96, 101, 104, 105, 107, 109, 110, 114, 116, 118, 122, 123, 124, 125, 126, 127, 128, 129, 130, 131, 132, 134, 135, 137, 139, 141, 142 Gina Amador

ILLUSTRATION SOURCES

Pp. 20, 21, 25, 33, 39, 40, 45 William H. Ukers, *All About Tea* (The Tea and Coffee Trade Journal, 1935)

RECIPE CREDITS

p. 56 *The Art of Easy Entertaining* (Cole Group, 1993); p. 73 Donna Lo Christy; p. 80 *Flavors of Japan* (Cole Group, 1988); p. 124 Gina Amador; p. 129 Bruce Hill

The REPUBLIC of TEA

The Republic of Tea is dedicated to finding and offering the finest teas and herbs on earth and to inspiring its citizens to enjoy life sip by sip, rather than gulp by gulp. The Republic was launched in 1992 and soared to national prominence with its extensive line of rare and unusual black, green, Oolong, and herbal teas, which are sold in more than 1,500 specialty food, gift, and department stores throughout North America and through a handsome mail-order catalog. The products and their packaging have been honored by The National Association of the Specialty Food Trade, *The Tea Quarterly* and *Fancy Food* magazines.

The story of the Republic's founding is related in ***The Republic of Tea: Letters to a Young Zentrepreneur*** (Doubleday/Currency, 1992), which the *Los Angeles Times* hailed as "one of the best business books of the year."

For information about where to purchase the leaves of The Republic of Tea, or for a copy of a mail-order catalog, please contact:

THE MINISTRY OF SUPPLY
2165 East Francisco Blvd. Suite E
San Rafael, California USA 94901
(415) 721-2170.